Cycling in North Wales

Philip Routledge

Published by Sigma Leisure – an imprint of
Sigma Press, 1 South Oak Lane, Wilmslow, Cheshire SK9 6AR, England.

British Library Cataloguing in Publication Data
A CIP record for this book is available from the British Library.

ISBN: 1-85058-472-9

Typesetting and Design by: Sigma Press, Wilmslow, Cheshire.

Cover photograph: Aberdaron, North Wales

Photographs and maps: the author

Printed by: MFP Design & Print

Disclaimer: the information in this book is given in good faith and is believed to be correct at the time of publication. No responsibility is accepted by either the author or publisher for errors or omissions, or for any loss or injury howsoever caused. Only you can judge your own fitness, competence and experience.

Preface

Cycling at a leisurely pace is the best way to explore North Wales. There are the added benefits of enhancing fitness both physically and mentally; leisure cycling is a pursuit which will bring joy to the heart of everybody who partakes. It is not an elitist activity and is open to literally anybody who is willing to sit on a bicycle and have a go at pushing the pedals.

This book takes you to a selection of routes in North Wales that offer this ideal. It points you in the right direction, offers a few titbits of local background interest and then leaves you free to enjoy yourself in a quiet and uncomplicated way. In addition to a range of simple half-day rides, there are some fine longer touring routes and a route which will enable even newcomers to cycling to make an ascent and descent of wild and wonderful Snowdon.

Each route has been chosen with a particular emphasis on introducing the cyclist to something more than just another bike ride. There is always something a little different, something that cannot be found anywhere else. As well as enjoying a pleasant cycle ride and a taking a sensible dose of healthy exercise, the cyclist will draw equal satisfaction from some other aspect of the outing. This may be an industrial archeological connection, a look at some rare wildlife or simply some particularly appealing view or beauty spot.

Every route in 'Cycling in North Wales' can be enjoyed by anyone who can ride a bike, from the novice to the super-fit sports rider and each route is guaranteed to produce a worthwhile return for the effort put in by the rider.

North Wales offers some dramatic scenery and some truly fascinating experiences. This new book shows you how to access the real landscape and enjoy it in the true spirit of leisure.

Philip Routledge

Contents

Introduction   1

The Rides

Ride 1   Llyn Alaw Reservoir, Anglesey   11
          Distance: *23 miles (37 km).*

Ride 2   Newborough Village, Anglesey   15
          Distance: *13½ miles (22 km).*

Ride 3   Newborough Forest, Anglesey   19
          Distance: *4 miles (6.5 km).*

Ride 4   Caernarfon Coast and Castle Ride   23
          Distance: *10½ miles (17 km).*

Ride 5   Lon Eifion, Caernarfon to Bryncir   27
          Distance: *28 miles (45 km).*

Ride 6   The Lleyn Peninsula   31
          Distance: *40 miles (64 km).*

Ride 7   To the Summit of Snowdon   37
          Distance: *20½ miles (33 km).*

Ride 8   Forestry Tracks in Beddgelert Forest   42
          Distance: *6 miles (9.5 km).*

Ride 9   The Valleys of Beddgelert   46
          Distance: *10½ miles (17 km).*

Ride 10   Great Orme's Head and Llandudno   50
          Distance: *7½ miles (12 km).*

Ride 11   **Conwy Castle**   **54**
Distance: *10½ miles (17 km).*

Ride 12   **Gwydyr Forest, Betws y Coed**   **58**
Distance: *6 or 9 miles. (9.5 or 14.5 km).*

Ride 13   **Clocaenog Forest**   **62**
Distance: *15 miles (24 km).*

Ride 14   **Denbigh Castle**   **66**
Distance: *7½ miles (12 km)*

Ride 15   **Ruabon Mountain and the Lead Mines of Coedpoeth**   **70**
Distance: *22½ miles (36 km)*

Ride 16   **The Llangollen Canal**   **74**
Distance: *11 miles (17.5 km)*

Ride 17   **The River Dee: Corwen to Llangollen**   **78**
Distance: *23 miles (37 km)*

Ride 18   **A Circuit of Llyn Tegid (Lake Bala)**   **82**
Distance: *13½ miles (21.5 km)*

Ride 19   **Bala and Llyn Celyn**   **86**
Distance: *19 miles (30.5 km)*

Ride 20   **The Afon Artro Valley: Shell Island to Llyn Cwm Bychan**   **90**
Distance: *17 miles (27 km)*

Ride 21   **Llanfachreth and Coed-y-Brenin Forest**   **94**
Distance: *8 miles (13 km)*

Ride 22   **Llanfachreth**   **98**
Distance: *6 miles (9.5 km)*

Ride 23   **The Morfa Mawddach Rail Path**   **102**
Distance: *16 miles (25.5 km)*

Ride 24   **Forest Trails in Coed-y-Brenin**   **106**
Distance: *7 miles (11 km)*

Ride 25   **Tywyn to Tal-y-Llyn (Llyn Mwyngil)**   **110**
Distances: *3 miles to 30 miles (5 km to 48 km)*

Ride 26   **Corris and the Dyfi forest**   **115**
Distance: *23 miles (37 km)*

Ride 27   **Lake Vyrnwy and Llanwddyn Village**   **119**
Distance: *12 miles (19 km)*

Ride 28   **Staylittle and Llyn Clywedog**   **123**
Distance: *19 miles (30.5 km)*

Ride 29   **Nant-y-Moch Reservoir and Anglers' Retreat**   **127**
Distance: *35 miles (56 km)*

Ride 30   **The Elan and Claerwen Valleys**   **131**
Distances: *23 miles (37 km) or 33 miles (53km)*

Ride 31   **A Long Tour of North Wales**   **135**
Distance: *300 miles (480 km)*

Welsh Place Names   **139**

Cycle Hirers in North Wales   **143**

Locations of Rides

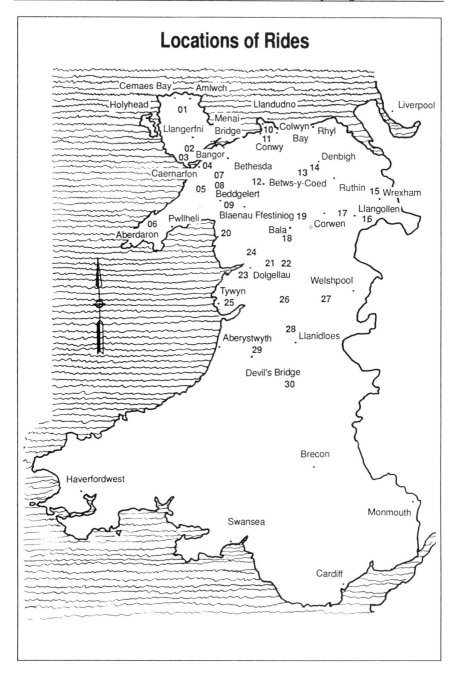

Introduction

The Seven Wonders of Wales

> "Pistyll Rhaiadr and Wrexham Steeple
> Snowdon's Mountain without its people
> Overton Yew Trees, St Winefride's Wells
> Llangollen Bridge and Gresford Bells."

Surely there are few places so diverse within so few square miles as North Wales and perhaps a glance at this famous old rhyme says it all. Take just the opening two lines: "Pystyll Rhaiadr", a spectacular 240-foot waterfall where North Wales literally falls over the historic border into England, "Wrexham Steeple" looking out over gently, rolling green fields that could be in virtually any region of patchwork Britain and then "Snowdon", wild, unpredictable, untamed and beautiful. There are also lakes, new and old, recent additions being created by massive spectacular dams which hold back billions of gallons of water in the deep 'V' formed valleys that are scattered around the region.

All this diversity makes for interesting, varied and very special cycling conditions and, when viewed in a little more detail, an ideal backcloth for this superb range of bicycle routes. Historically, North Wales has always been a popular cycle touring venue, but with traffic building up over recent years and the vast increase in demand for family cycling routes, this book is designed to guide you away from traffic and show you how to get the best out of this fantastic scenery without busting a gut or competing for space with articulated lorries.

When most people think of North Wales, one of the first images to spring to mind is that of mountainous scenery. There are a lot of mountains in North Wales but there are also a lot of valleys, a lot of rivers, a lot of lakes and a lot of coastline. By combining all the facets of the topography into a range of carefully devised and sensibly balanced cycling routes, this book has something for everyone.

Using the book is simple. Chose your route and turn to the relevant pages for instructions, directions and background information. Once you have decided, check the weather forecast, plan your time and get out there and enjoy your cycling.

Equipment

☐ Additional equipment translates to additional weight.

☐ Additional weight translates to additional effort.

☐ Hills, especially upward hills, and head winds magnify the undesirable effects of additional weight.

Bearing these simple rules in mind and on the assumption that your bike has pedals, wheels and security equipment, there are really only a few simple accessories that are worth considering. These are as follows:

The **bell** might well be fitted to your bike anyway. If not, don't worry. You can always sing, cough or loudly clear your throat, but a bell is easier. It is associated with cycling and it is inoffensive.

The **frame corner pack** is useful because it is dedicated to carrying your **puncture kit**, basic **tool kit** and **first aid** equipment. Once it is packed, you can forget about it but it will be there when needed. Keep the tools to a minimum. On most bikes two Allen keys, a multi spanner and a cross head screw driver are sufficient.

Your puncture repair kit is not much use without a **pump**.

A Back (or Front) Rack: a rack is so useful, I don't know how people manage without.

A Single or Double Lightweight Pannier: Panniers in either single or double form enable you to carry spare clothing, sandwiches, cool drinks, and anything else which you may require.

A Front Mud/Spray Deflector: You'll know why you need a front spray deflector the first time you try to ride on a wet or muddy surface.

Security

A Sad Story: lock it or lose it – and don't leave it outside at night. If you are leaving your bike out of sight, particularly in towns and cities, **do** lock it or you **will** lose it. It is a sad state of affairs, but according to crime prevention statistics, the chances of an un-guarded and unlocked bicycle being stolen in the busy central area of a town the size of Swindon would be greater than 50% over a 48 hour period. The chances of a **locked** but unguarded bicycle being vandalised or having pieces taken off it (like wheels!) during periods of darkness are greater than 30% over the same period.

In other words, you are more likely to lose your bike than you are not to lose it, so here are a few simple tips.

☐ Use a D-lock around the frame, through the rear wheel and onto the most solid object you can find. A lot of towns and cities now have proper cycle parking arrangements. Most commonly these are Sheffield Stands, strong n-shaped metal stands which are specially designed for bicycle locking. If possible, secure your front wheel, even if it means carrying another locking device.

☐ Make sure that you have a photograph of your bicycle and a note of any serial numbers or distinctive markings and carry this with you. Use special invisible ultra-violet markers and write your name or postcode on the bike. By doing this and having the descriptive information readily available, at least you can give the police a chance.

☐ Just in case the worst does happen, always make sure you are carrying your bus fare to get home. A long walk after the indignation of losing your bike will dim even the brightest spirit.

Safety

☐ Keep off busy roads whenever possible.

☐ Be Safe, Be Seen. Lights at night. Fluorescents by day.

☐ Ring Your Bell when approaching pedestrians.

☐ Wear Helmets for rough, off-road riding.

☐ Make sure that your bicycle is properly maintained.

Buying a Bicycle

Apart from colour and budget, there are some deciding factors when buying a bicycle and these notes will hopefully offer a few tips.

The correct type of machine for you and your budget: there are several clearly definable types of bicycle and each has its own particular advantages and disadvantages. Here is a brief list of the major options along with the pros and cons of various categories.

Mountain Bike (also known as MTB or ATB): *Pro:* Go anywhere. Very easy to ride, very manoeuvrable. *Con:* Poor for long distance touring or speed work.

Roadster (the traditional vicar's bike): *Pro:* Solid, hub gears. Will probably last for ever. *Con:* Heavy and very hard to pedal up hill, which is probably why vicars usually push.

Shopper (small-wheeled lightweight bicycle, mainly for the ladies): *Pro:* Easy to ride, easy to store. Hardly ever stolen. *Con:* No good off-road and not much better on-road.

Folding Bike (one for the boater?): *Pro:* Transportable in tiny spaces such as car boots, canal boats, yacht tenders, buses or trains. Great for the urban jungle. *Con:* Limited in its overall ability by its tiny wheels and compromised design.

Quality Touring Bicycle: (often seen loaded with panniers): *Pro:* A quality touring bicycle is a joy to ride and a joy to own. Long distance riding can be carried out in comfort. The best all-round bicycle to own. *Con:* Quality does not come cheap. Really rough stuff should be left to the ATB's.

Hybrid (half mountain bike, half tourer): *Pro:* Lighter and more comfortable than a mountain bike. Better on tarmac *Con:* Limited off-road ability.

Sporting Bicycle (thin-rimmed wheels, drop bars): *Pro:* Can be faster than a tourer. *Con:* Not as comfortable or as strong as a tourer. Horrible on anything but billiard table surfaces.

Road Racing Bicycles (thin-rimmed wheels, quality lightweight frames): *Pro:* Ultimate speed depends how much you are willing to pay. Expensive, specialist racing bicycles are a joy to behold. *Con:* Unless you are road racing or training for road racing, these machines are useless.

Owning a Bicycle

Owning a bicycle should be a great pleasure and a good bicycle, well maintained and well cared for will prove to be a friend for life. Like most things, ownership of a bicycle can be as expensive or as cheap as you care to make it.

Service Schedules: If you are using your bicycle regularly and you are not confident in carrying out your own servicing, an annual service at a reputable cycle dealer is a great investment.

Insurance: Insurance is very much a matter of personal choice and personal circumstance. It is not compulsory and often you will be buying cover that you already have in another form. If you have one, check the terms of your house insurance policy and look into the possibility of paying a small extra premium for your cycling needs.

Cleaning: By cleaning your bicycle regularly you will achieve three things. Firstly it will look better, secondly it will operate more smoothly and thirdly you will become aware of faults before they develop into serious problems. Use warm soapy water and be certain to oil the chain and gears after the water has dried off. Wash carefully around the brakes and around the gear sets.

The Cyclist's Essential Check List

It is good practice to carry out the following quick checks each time you set out.

- ☐ **Tyres.** Inflated, good tread.
- ☐ **Tools.** Basic appropriate tools carried plus the pump.
- ☐ **Adjustments.** Are the saddle and the handlebars set at the correct height and rake?
- ☐ **Spare tube** and puncture repair kit.
- ☐ **Security.** D-lock or good chain carried.
- ☐ **Lubrication.** Have you oiled your chain recently? Every fifty miles, after washing or rain or every two weeks when in use.
- ☐ **Lights.** Will you need them?
- ☐ **Ingredients.** Food and water if required.

☐ **Clothing.** Check the weather.

☐ **Condition of the bicycle.** A final look over your bicycle. Check your steering, brakes and gears.

Insects, Sun and Wind

Insects: a good insect repellent is an essential requirement, especially on hot summer days.

Sun: take the appropriate precautions of sun protection cream.

Wind: Do not underestimate the effect of the wind. A good tailwind can take a great deal of the effort out of cycling; a strong headwind, conversely, will require much greater effort than still wind conditions. If you are planning to cycle and return along the same leg, tackle the upwind direction first and you will then be able to look forward to an easier return trip.

Dress Sense

If you are likely to be riding along busy roads, in towns or at night, make sure you can be seen – wear a brightly-coloured cycle helmet, shirt, anorak etc.

In rain, there are two schools of thought and depending on which one you subscribe to you will either get wet or you will get hot. The decision to put on waterproofs or get wet is always difficult to get right and initially, if you undecided, always put the waterproofs on as soon as the rain starts because once you are wet, the waterproofs will only hold the moisture in.

Hiring

The wide availability of cycle hire centres has happily created a situation whereby you do not need to own a bicycle to enjoy the routes in this book. Use some basic common sense when hiring and consider the following points:

Charges. It is up to you to decide if the charges are fair or not, but do be sure that you know exactly what you are expected to pay. Some hirers quote by the hour, some by the day and some by the week, so take care. Shop around if you can.

Deposits. Do not leave your car keys. Effectively, your car is held as a deposit and this is disproportionate. All hirers will, quite reasonably, insist on some form of identification. A driving licence, a credit card or a passport are usually acceptable either solely or in combination.

Transporting Your Bicycle By Car

There are several methods and each has pros and cons:

Roof rack clamp fittings. *Pro:* Security, less possibility of damage to the bicycle. *Con:* Low bridges. putting the bicycle on and taking it off.

Back Rack. *Pro:* Very easy to use. Cheap to buy. *Con:* Poor security when the car is unattended. Can knock the bicycles about if you are carrying more than one.

Tow Bar Rack. *Pro:* Good security, you can D-lock your bike to your car. Ease of use. *Con:* You need a towbar.

There are pitfalls to beware of. Here are a few:

☐ If you have any fast-fix, clip-on equipment such as pumps, drinking bottles, mudguards, pannier sets or anything else that is not welded or screwed to the bicycle, take it off or it will certainly fall off.

☐ If you are carrying your bikes on a roof rack, beware of car park barriers.

☐ Bicycles carried transversely on racks on the backs of the cars are generally wider than the car itself. If you are travelling along narrow lanes or through tight town streets, allow for that extra bit of width.

☐ If you are transporting your bicycle on a back rack, make certain that your bicycle tyres are well clear of the car's exhaust. The hot exhaust gases can melt the tyre.

Note that these are generally illegal in Europe because number-plates are obscured; users may find themselves being heavily fined!

Railways, Buses and Aeroplanes

Two of the pleasure cyclist's greatest allies are the tailwind and the downward gradient. Unfortunately some of the basic laws of mathematics and geometry dictate that whatever goes up must come down and whatever blows one one way does not blow back the other way half an hour later when you happen to want to return. The answer to your dilemma may well lie in a bit of pre-planning and a railway station or a bus stop.

Railway Travel: The services offered to cyclists by train operators are constantly changing, especially in view of the turmoil of reorganisation within the railway industry. For latest information check before you plan to travel and always expect to book because space is limited. In broad terms, most train operators are helpful and well-disposed towards cyclists but demand can be high.

On journeys where changes of train are required, you will normally be expected to be responsible for moving your own bicycle but this would probably be advisable under any circumstances. Remember these rules and you should be OK:

☐ Book before you go. (There may be a £3 fee)

☐ Long distance trains such as sleeper services and Intercity services will have an overall capacity for forty bicycles.

☐ 'Sprinters' have space for four bicycles per pair of carriages.

If in doubt, keep smiling because conductors have discretion beyond these limits if space allows.

Bus Travel: Buses are best used to 'get back home' or 'get back to a parked car' having secured your bicycle in some safe place for later retrieval. It is an easy job to check local services and timetables and plan a day's cycling on this basis and it is a fantastic way to use a good tailwind!

Facilities offered by bus operators for carrying bicycles by bus tend to be fairly sketchy in terms of both detail and availability. There are however a few facilities available for bicycles. In these cases, the costs are usually very high although some operators actually offer free passage for bicycles. In all cases enquiry and pre-booking are essential.

Air Travel: Most major airlines will carry bicycles either within your luggage allowance or at a small additional charge. Some airlines supply special bags free of charge. On pressurised aircraft, ensure that you deflate the tyres otherwise they may explode at altitude due to the low atmospheric pressure in the hold.

Summary: There is a vast range of transport services on offer for cyclists within the public domain but availability is almost always subject to booking. The golden rule is simple. Book and enquire before travelling!

Common Notices and Waymarks

There is a multitude of information available to cyclists in the form of waymarks and notices. These can be rings or signs, fixed to the street furniture, or they can be bits of painted wood, nailed to walls or wired to trees. There are waymarks carved in stone, painted on the tarmac, stencilled onto wood, routed into posts and set in concrete and there are all combinations of styles and materials. I am sure that these are not the only forms that I have seen on my travels, but it will give you an idea.

It would be nice to believe that waymarking of any particular route is consistent in its format and presentation but be warned, it is not. Just because you have seen a run of twelve wooden posts with yellow tops and a routed message saying 'Cycle Path' does not mean that the next post is not blue concrete with the message 'Bikes' and buried in the back of the hedge. Beware of practical jokers who take delight in turning pointers to send you the wrong way, and try to verify the route, especially in or near urban areas where petty vandalism may occur.

Keep a constant lookout for waymarks and try to find a pattern, as it will greatly enhance your enjoyment of the ride. If you do come across any vandalism, try to report it to the responsible authority so that they may include the problem in their work schedules.

Rights of Way

In Wales, you are forbidden access to land unless you are granted some right waiving the landowner's rights. This may come in the form of a public footpath, a bridle way, a highway or a permissive route. Canal towpaths and most railway paths are good examples of permissive routes.

Generally, common sense will guide you along if you lose the way. If in doubt, keep to well used and established paths, look out for evidence of cycle tracks and follow your front wheel.

Ride 1

Llyn Alaw Reservoir, Anglesey

A gentle ride via very quiet country lanes around the Llyn Reservoir in the central area of Anglesey

Maps: Landranger 1:50,000 series. Sheet numbers 114

Distance: 23 miles (37 km)

374857

Waymarked: No

Gradients: Nothing that will cause any great difficulty

Surface: Tarmac country lanes

Future Proposals: N/A

Other Cycle Routes Linking: None

Bicycle Hire: Caernarfon, Beaumaris, Menai Bridge

Shops and Refreshments: Llanerchymedd, otherwise, take your own provisions

Special Comments: N/A

Special Warnings: N/A

Permits: N/A

Unspoilt Anglesey is a delightful haven of peace. Inland there are numerous small whitewashed farms and cottages with stone walls around tiny fields. On the craggy coast are dunes, cliffs and lovely small sandy beaches. Few places have more prehistoric monuments and the bridges to the mainland, built by Telford and Stephenson, are famous in their own right.

Llyn Alaw (the lake in the valley) is situated in the peaceful and unspoilt central area of Anglesey, an area often ignored by the mainstream tourist. The drystone walls, slabs of exposed bedrock in the fields, low banked medieval grass mounds and an ancient patchwork field pattern create a scene reminiscent of a time in the past. The ride gently undulates along little lanes with grass centres and parallel tarmac strips.

Llyn Alaw is a recently constructed reservoir serving the local

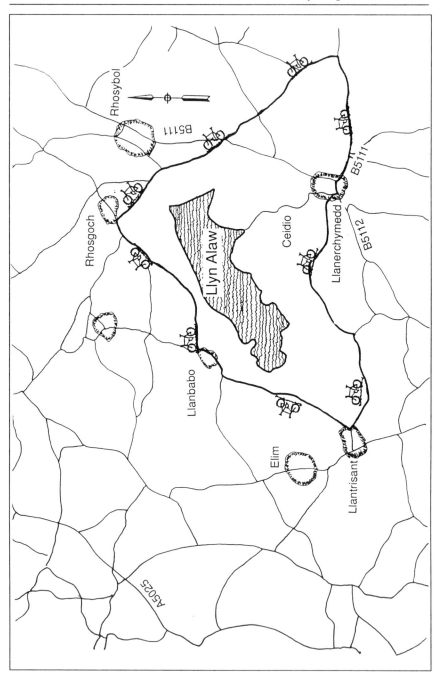

community and supplying cooling for a small power station. Where the valley was once an unmanageable marsh it is now a beautiful four-mile stretch of water. The distant views over the peaceful Anglesey landscape are charming on a summer's day.

The ride takes a route in a rough circle around the lake. There are some great picnic spots, official and unofficial. If you are keen on bird watching take some binoculars or if you are an angler take a rod. For both activities, there are some good opportunities around the visitor centre.

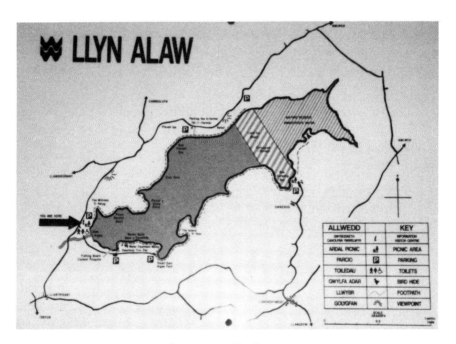

Access Points

The ride begins and ends at the visitor centre on the north-west corner of Llyn Alaw's dam. From Amlwch, take the Rhosgoch road and after passing through the village, pass to the north of Llyn Alaw to reach the visitor centre car park.

The Route

1. From the visitor car park on the north-west corner of the dam, turn left.

2. Follow the country lane in a south-westerly direction. After ¼ of a mile turn left onto a southerly heading.

3. Follow this lane for 2½ miles to the T-junction.

4. Turn left at the T-junction and follow the lane for a mile and half in an easterly direction.

5. At the next T-junction turn left and follow the road to the outskirts of the village of Llechcynfarwy.

6. Turn right and then left along the B5112 in the village.

7. After twenty yards turn right along the B5111 and continue out of the village for fifty yards. These few yards are the busiest of the ride and some care should be taken.

8. Take the first left-hand turn to rejoin the minor road system and continue east for one mile before turning left at the crossroads to head north-west.

9. At the crossroads with B5111 continue straight ahead for three miles passing two minor turnings to the right.

10. At the crossroads turn left to head south-west and continue to return to the visitor centre.

Nearby

Amlwch on the north coast is a delightful coastal resort, well worth a visit. Parys Mountain is situated some two miles south of Amlwch, a weird and wonderful moonscape, originally a copper mine which also yielded other treasures including sulphur, alum, zinc and silver. Here is a scene which would be an ideal film set for a holocaust movie. A mixture of poisoned barren waste deposits, ivy growing from nowhere and camouflaging remains of old engine stacks, a windmill stump and long-disused cottages certainly create an eerie atmosphere. Copper-coloured pools and jagged shadows enhance this effect at sunset.

Ride 2

Newborough Village, Anglesey

A ride through very quiet country lanes in the plains north-west of Newborough. Very pleasant cycling and hardly any adverse gradient.

Maps: Landranger 1:50,000 series. Sheet number 114

Distance: 13½ miles (22 km)

Waymarked: No

Gradients: Nothing uphill which should upset you too much

Surface: Tarmac lanes, sometimes with grassy centres

Future Proposals: N/A

Other Cycle Routes Linking: Ride 3 (Newborough Forest)

Bicycle Hire: Caernarfon

Shops and Refreshments: Newborough

Special Comments: N/A

Special Warnings: N/A

Permits: N/A

This is a lovely ride through quiet and virtually traffic-free lanes in the marsh plain areas north-east of the peaceful villages of Newborough and Malltraeth. The Malltraeth Marsh (Cors Ddyga) area is drained by the Afon Cefni which runs towards the sea behind great flood banks. The little lanes are a haven of wildlife and rich with wild flowers and a profusion of summer berries which offer a veritable feast at the right time of year.

There is a short section of the route which follows the main A4080 but a good alternative parallel way exists along a raised (sea defence) footpath and via vehicular forestry trails on the edge of Newborough Forest. The seaward 'landscapes' vary tremendously under different conditions of tide and keen bird watchers can spend hours studying the comings, goings, feeding patterns and general movements of a vast range of birds.

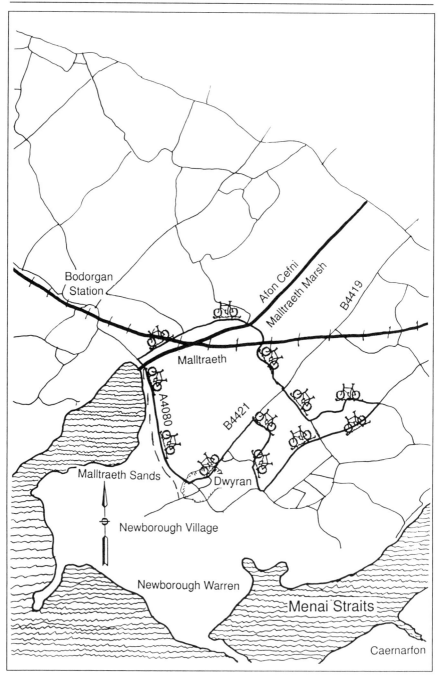

For a bit of 'fun' cycling, you may wish to lose yourself in Newborough Forest (See ride 3.) It offers a great choice of easy forestry tracks which will suit families and non-sporting riders. There are plenty of tracks in the forest, all guaranteeing beautifully wild surroundings and the possibility of great views. Most are gentle and undemanding, ideal for those who just prefer to potter along and enjoy the surroundings.

Access Points

The starting point of the ride is from the centre of Newborough village, but you could start from anywhere along the route. Mall-traeth would be a good alternative and many cyclists will prefer the prospect of starting their day's riding by getting the worst 'A' road section out of the way (while all of the family are paying attention?) The directions are given in an anti-clockwise direction to avoid as many right-hand turns as possible.

A tunnel of trees just outside Newborough

The Route

1. From the centre of Newborough village, take the B4421 signed to Llangaffo.

2. Leave the village past the school and continue straight ahead along the long flat road for 1½ miles before turning right into a very minor lane, just past a row of houses.

3. Follow this lane as it winds around for about a mile and at the subsequent T-junction, turn left.

4. At the junction with A4080 go straight ahead for just 20 yards before taking the left turn just by the garage.

5. Carry straight ahead at the next crossroads (the B4419).

6. At the next (staggered) crossroads, turn left and follow this road to the T-junction with the B4419.

7. Turn right along the B4419.

8. Go straight across the B4421 in the village of Llangaffo (slightly right then left).

9. Follow this road out of the village, under the railway and over the hump bridge crossing Afon Cefni.

10. Turn left over the bridge signed to Malltraeth and follow under the railway viaduct towards the coast.

11. In Malltraeth, turn left over the bridge to return to Newborough. There is an alternative footpath route along a tidal causeway which subsequently leads to forestry tracks. This is commonly used by local cyclists.

Nearby

The A4080 coast road is around 20 miles (16 km) long and enjoys marvellous views from virtually every inch of its length. Although it is classified as an 'A' road, it does not carry the weight of traffic which is more normally associated with this classification. The going is easy, the surface is good and there are plenty of pleasant stopping-off places. There are also plenty of roads running down to the coast as well as little lanes running inland.

Ride 3

Newborough Forest, Anglesey

A very short ride into the forest allowing you a toll-free visit to the fabulous cool pine woods and dunes along the edge of the Menai Straits. A great way to make the best of your bicycle.

Maps: Landranger 1:50,000 series. Sheet numbers 114

Distance: 4 miles (6.5 km)

Waymarked: No. Follow the forest toll road to the car park

Gradients: None worth mentioning

Surface: Tarmac or solid forest track if you decide to take an excursion into the woods. Avoid drifting sand or sandy paths. They are virtually impossible to ride along.

Future Proposals: N/A

Other Cycle Routes Linking: Ride 2. Country lanes out of Newborough village

Bicycle Hire: Caernarfon

Shops and Refreshments: Newborough village

Special Comments: N/A

Special Warnings: N/A

Permits: N/A

This short ride takes advantage of one of the bicycle's greatest assets, its ability to avoid traffic queues, and the freedom of toll-free access to forestry property. The toll road into Newborough Forest gives access to lovely dunes, pine woods and beach facilities as well as the Warren nature reserve and further access to the maze of forestry roads which lace through the conifer woodland. The road into the forest is passable by car if drivers are willing to queue for privilege of passing over a ground barrier that would stop a tank (but not a bicycle), and push several substantial pieces of eight down the throat of an unsmiling toll machine.

Cyclists may ride straight past the queue of cars, while whistling a happy tune and enjoy a delightful toll-free ride through the woods without fear of retribution or parking problems on a busy bank

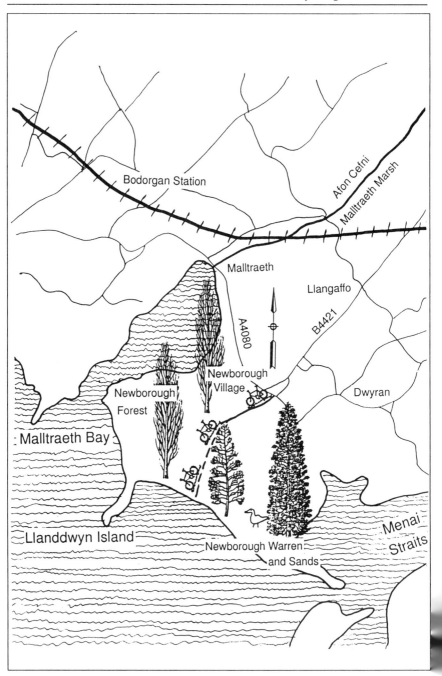

holiday. In addition, there are plenty of vehicular forestry trails which are ideal for cycling, as long as you avoid sandy tracks, footpaths and areas reserved for nature.

The Newborough Warren National Nature Reserve which adjoins the forest covers 1500 acres of open sand dunes. The predominant bird species are waders such as the noisy oystercatchers, redshanks and curlews (the largest wading birds). In addition, powerful peregrine falcons, and various breeds of sandpiper patrol the foreshore and feed on the rich stocks of unwary fish.

The sands on the edge of Newborough Forest

Access Points

Access the forest from Newborough village signed to 'Traith' or 'Beach'. Go past the toll machine and tank barrier and follow the tarmac road through the forest to the large car parking area.

The Route

There are several vehicular forest roads within the area. The idea of this short ride is to avoid traffic and toll penalties within Newborough Forest (also better for the forest environment). Simply follow the access route instructions and use your common sense regarding forestry trails. Footpaths are no-go areas for cyclists in Newborough and although the forestry commission does not have a cycling policy within Newborough, their overall policy allows cycling along any vehicular forestry road system. Note the warnings regarding sandy paths.

Nearby

To the north-west of Newborough is Aberffraw and Aberffraw dunes. There are some great little lanes in this vicinity which offer good safe family cycling conditions. From the north-west corner of Newborough forest to Malltraeth is an interesting breakwater causeway which is used regularly by local cyclists as an alternative to the sometimes busy A4080. Although no information regarding cyclist's rights is available for this stretch, off-road riding is always preferable when the alternative is mixing with fast moving traffic, especially where family groups are concerned.

Ride 4

Caernarfon Coast and Castle Ride

*A charming figure-of-eight ride based on Caernarfon Castle,
following a quiet lane along the waters edge of the Menai Straits
and returning to Caernarfon along a section of the Lon Eifion
purpose-built railway path.*

Maps: Landranger 1:50,000 series. Sheet number 115

Distance: 10½ miles (17 km)

Waymarked: No

Gradients: Hardly worth mentioning

Surface: Tarmac

Future Proposals: N/A

Other Cycle Routes Linking: Ride 5 (Lon Eifion Railway Path to Bryncir)

Bicycle Hire: Caernarfon

Shops and Refreshments: Caernarfon

Special Comments: N/A

Special Warnings: N/A

Permits: N/A

This is a lovely ride with a high degree of interest combined with
waterside lanes and great views. If you have an interest in birds,
there are few places better suited to spotting a wide range of sea birds
particularly divers and waders who will entertain you with their fish
catching skills. If you simply enjoy enjoy the seaside, here you have
some lovely unspoilt coastline. If you enjoy very easy problem-free
and virtually traffic-free cycling conditions, this is an ideal family
ride.

The whole route is dominated by the presence of the Menai
Straits and the unusually close proximity of Anglesey which at times
you may feel is within wading range over the narrow (but deep)
stretch of water. The ride traverses the coastline and follows the
sand and shingle shore as it runs inland at the magical inlet of Foryd

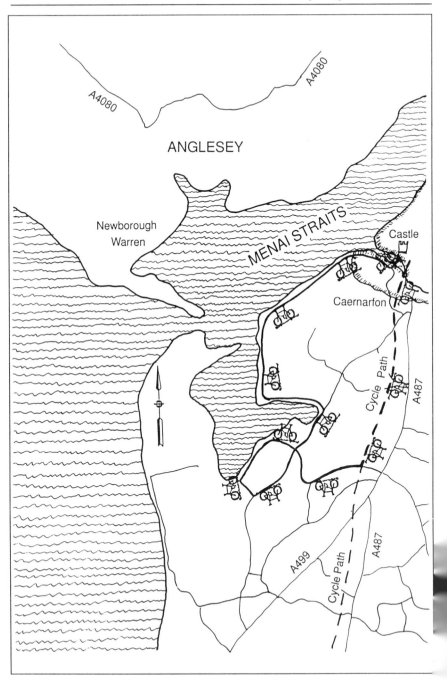

Bay. On a calm day there is beauty all around, on a windswept day, this can be a wild and exiting place to be.

Caernarfon Castle is the starting point for this ride and if you have time, it is well worth a visit. If you do nothing else, marvel at the sheer thickness of the walls and the massive presence of the place. The footbridge which crosses the Afon Seiont opposite the castle and forms the start of the ride.

Access Points

Start the ride by crossing the Aber Footbridge opposite the entrance to Caernarfon Castle. There are several good car parks in the town including the old rail yard which forms the end of the Lon Eifion Railway Path. As part of the ride, make a point of exploring Caernarfon, especially the old town area north of the castle.

The footbridge to Caernarfon Castle

The Route

1. Cross the Aber Footbridge opposite the entrance to Caernarfon Castle and turn right to ride along parallel to the river with the water on your right.

2. Continue to follow this road along the waters edge of the Menai Straits where Anglesey will appear to be tantalisingly close. Continue around the eastern edge of Foryd Bay until the road turns inland and arrives at a T-junction.

3. Turn right at the T-junction and continue through the village of Saron.

4. Immediately after passing through the village, take the first right back towards Foryd Bay at the crossroads. (You will return to these crossroads shortly so turn left here for a short cut).

5. Follow this little road around until you come to a T-junction.

6. Turn left here and continue until you arrive back at the crossroads on the edge of Saron.

7. Turn right at the crossroads this time signed to Dinas.

8. After passing some houses fork left towards the church signed to Lon Eifion.

9. Turn left along the Lon Eifion Railway Path to return to Caernarfon

Nearby

Caernarfon Castle was the venue of Prince Charles' investiture in 1969. In 1963 Queen Elizabeth ll made Caernarfon a Royal Borough and since the reorganisation of local government in 1974, it has been a royal town.

Twthill is a rocky outcrop situated half a mile north-east of the old town and is well worth visiting on a clear day to enjoy the superb views of Snowdonia, the Menai Straits, Anglesey and Caernarfon Castle.

The Queen's Tower, named after Eleanor, wife of Edward l, contains the museum of the Royal Welsh Fusiliers Regiment. The display which covers three floors includes no less than eight Victoria Cross Medals.

Ride 5

Lon Eifion, Caernarfon to Bryncir

A great railway path ride along the old track bed of the Caernarfon to Criccieth railway.

Maps: Landranger 1:50,000 series. Sheet numbers 123 and 115

Distance: 28 miles (45 km)

Waymarked: Yes

Gradients: None. (old railway track bed)

Surface: Solid and well-drained

Future Proposals: To extend the ride south at Bryncir

Other Cycle Routes Linking: Ride 4 (Based on Caernarfon Castle and Menai Straits)

Bicycle Hire: Caernarfon

Shops and Refreshments: Caernarfon, Pen-y-groes and Bryncir plus other villages along the route

Special Comments: N/A

Special Warnings: N/A

Permits: N/A

This virtually flat railway trail enjoys solid, smooth and well-drained surfaces. The route is varied and interesting in both wildlife and industrial archaeological senses. It offers the complete ingredients for pleasurable traffic-free cycling, all set in the magnificence of some of the most beautiful river valleys and estuaries of this most scenic region of North Wales.

The path's surface is purpose-built for cycling, walking and movement of wheelchairs and because of its railway origins, enjoys level gradients and a well-drained substructure. It offers a clear 14 mile (24km) stretch of easy, traffic-free cycling, all on a consolidated surface, where both the novice cyclist or the hardened enthusiast can capture equal pleasure. A novice rider should easily and comfortably cover the route one way in under two hours' cycling.

Historically, the railway carried slate from the Nantile quarries and in more recent times, countless holidaymakers, many from the heavily industrialised Lancashire cotton towns, on their way to Butlin's holiday camp in Pwllheli. Originally the line was owned by the London Midland and Scottish Railway Company and ran from Bangor to Afon Wen. The cycle route begins and ends under the historic walls of Caernarfon Castle and passes through some glorious countryside.

Access Points

There are plenty of good access points throughout the route. The following list is not complete but it will offer suggestions to cover the route.

1. Caernarfon, in the centre (disguised as a car park!)

2. Bontnewydd, west of A499.

3. Glan-rhyd/Llanwnda, crossing the A499.

4. Groeslon, west of the A487(T).

5. Penygroes, west of the A487(T).

6. Llanllyfni, west of the A487(T).

7. Pant Glas, west of the A487(T).

8. Bryncir, an old railway yard west of the A487(T).

The Route

Because of the surrounding topography and the heavy traffic on the surrounding road system in the direct area, the full length of this cycle path should be best enjoyed as a traffic free return trip. After joining the cycle path in Bryncir or in Caernarfon, simply follow the waymarked route. The whole route is well-signed and very easy to follow. You will not need detailed directions but here are a few guidelines.

1.   From Caernarfon on the first part of the route heading south, you will soon bridge over the Afon Gwyrfai and then cross the A489 (follow the signs) south of Llanwnda where you will also pass the old interchange station with the narrow-gauge Welsh Highland line.

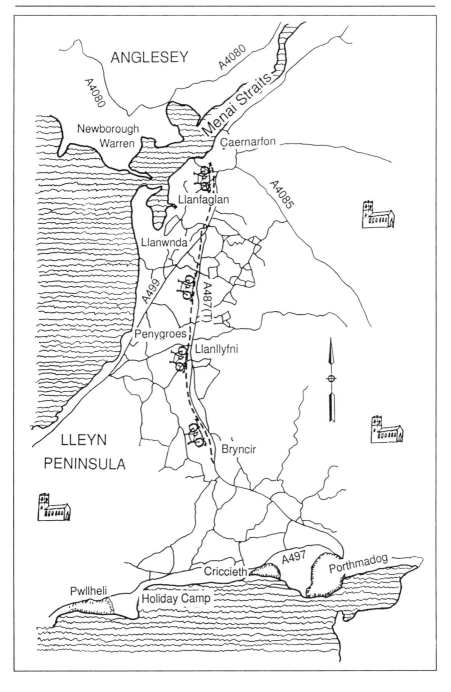

2. At Groeslon you will pass under a road bridge where there are still signs of the old mineral tramway that once followed this route.

3. After passing under another road bridge you will arrive at the village of Penygroes.

4. The route continues south, faithfully following the not-so-distant sound of the A487 (T) Caernarfon to Porthmadog road. There is high ground to the right beyond Llanllyfni.

5. After arriving at Bryncir, it is possible to continue to Criccieth along quiet country lanes.

Nearby

Caernarfon was an extremely well-defended town. The building of Caernarfon Castle was commenced by Edward I in 1283. It is one of the noblest ruins in Britain having walls 7 to 9 feet thick which, not surprisingly perhaps, are still entire. These enclose an oblong of three acres. There are thirteen embattled towers with five, six or eight sides and surmounted by turrets. The gateway under the great square tower has four portcullises. The town of Caernarfon was once surrounded itself by walls and round towers. These walls, with several of the gates, still exist, but are now within the town.

Ride 6

The Lleyn Peninsula

A superb full-day, 40-mile tour around the peaceful minor roads of the beautiful and unspoilt Lleyn Peninsula.

Maps: Landranger 1:50,000 series. Sheet number 123

Distance: 40 miles (64 km)

Waymarked: No

Gradients: Nothing too serious to worry about. The most severe section is just by Hell's Mouth. There are plenty of short climbs and plenty of descents to compensate.

Surface: Tarmac minor road, some with grass centre strip

Future Proposals: N/A

Other Cycle Routes Linking: N/A

Bicycle Hire: Pwllheli

Shops and Refreshments: Plenty of village shops and pubs along the route

Special Comments: N/A

Special Warnings: All of the route is on public roads. Take the proper 'Be seen' precautions

Permits: N/A

The little lanes of the Lleyn Peninsula are amongst the most peaceful in the whole of North Wales. This ride combines all of the essential ingredients for a good 40-mile tour and offers them by the bucket full. Plenty of villages, good wind shelter, no very serious gradients, low traffic density, great views, plenty of interest and the sea.

The Lleyn Peninsula offers spectacularly rocky coastline which plays a large part in forming the character of this ride. The route heads west along the north coast of the peninsula before turning at the lovely little village of Aberdaron to head east to Pwllheli where the ride begins and ends. While Pwllheli is considered to be one of the most sheltered harbours in North Wales, Aberdaron is one of the most treacherous.

Historically, the Lleyn Peninsula has been described as the land

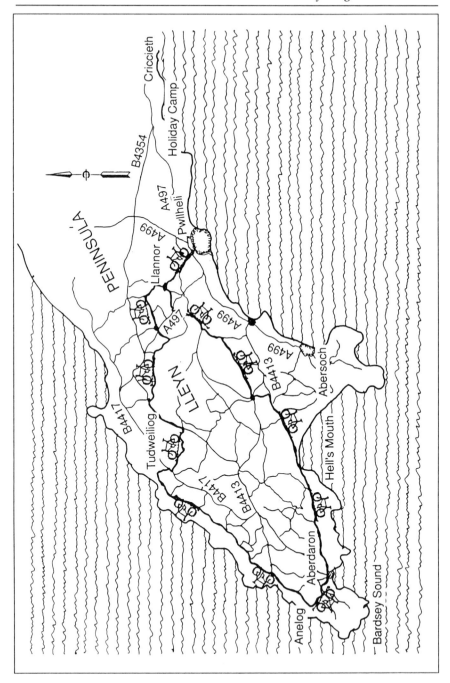

of missionaries, hostile invaders and pious pilgrims. Every church recalls some Celtic saint and marks a stage upon the pilgrim trail to Bardsey Island which stands in all its holiness and isolation a mile and a half across Bardsey Sound at the western most point of the peninsula.

Access Points

Hell's Mouth, at nearby Abersoch

The route is based on Pwllheli and the directions are given from the railway station near the town centre. There are plenty of car parks in and around Pwllheli although in the height of summer it is a matter of finding one with a space. If parking is a problem, a good alternative starting point would be the village of Llannor, a couple of miles north of Pwllheli.

The Route

1. From the station head towards the centre of Pwllheli. After a very short distance turn right into the main town at the mini island and carry straight ahead, keeping left. Follow signs to Llannor.

2. Turn right in Llannor village, leaving the church on your right.

3. Keep left at the fork between the two low stone walls.

4. Turn left at the next junction.

5. Take the second right just before a sharp left bend in front of a stone cottage. This will take you into a tree-tunnelled leafy lane with mossy stone walls either side.

6. Turn left at the T-junction along the B4354.

7. Go left at the junction with the A497 and then almost immediately turn right along the minor road.

8. Keep right at the junction and then right again at the next one.

9. Keep right at the next junction and then straight ahead at the cross roads signed to Edern.

10. Go straight on at the first left to pass Peniel Chapel. At the cross roads beyond, go left.

11. Follow this road for some distance before going right at the cross roads signed to Tudweiliog.

12. Follow this road to the B4417 at Tudweiliog and turn right.

13. Just beyond the edge of the village of Tudweiliog, turn left signed to the Beach.

14. Follow this road as it bends left to follow the coast past Porth Towyn.

15. Go right at the next three-way junction towards the sea.

16. Continue to follow the road as it tracks along the north coast.

17. At the sharp left-hand bend by the house 'Pen-y-gongi' and by a pebble-dashed bungalow, take the lane to the right between two high hedges.

18. At another sharp left-hand corner, facing a high hedge and a white house, go right to pass the house 'Tynlon' on your left. Turn left at the T-junction opposite the footpath to Porth Wydlin go left.

19. Continue to follow the road as it bends and twists to run parallel with the coastline.

20. At the T-junction go right signed to Aberdaron and Uwchmynydd.

21. At Anelog, where the road bends left, continue to follow the signs to Aberdaron.

22. At the cross roads at the edge of Aberdaron, continue straight on into the village.

23. At the next T-junction, facing the sea, turn left into the village of Aberdaron. Go right at the next T-junction in the village.

24. Follow out of the village with church and cemetery on your right.

25. Continue through the village of Y Rhiw and follow the signs to Abersoch and Pwllheli.

26. After passing the western tip of Hell's Mouth Bay, follow the road inland.

27. After crossing the causeway, follow the road around to right signed to Abersoch and Mynytho.

28. At the next crossroads carry straight on and shortly afterwards take the turn, slightly uphill to the left.

29. At the T-junction with the B4413, turn right.

30. After a short distance, where the road bends around to the right, carry straight on (left away from through route) uphill past the chapel on your left.

31. Follow this road between the beacons of Garn Bach and Garn Sacthon.

32. Turn left at the T-junction signed to 'Rhyd-y-clafdy'.

33. Turn right in the village onto the B4415.

34. Just after leaving the village, turn left into a narrow lane.

35. Carry straight on at the crossroads and then turn right along the A497.

36. After a short distance turn left and go left at the next junction to return to Llannor.

37. Turn right by the church in Llannor to retrace your track to Pwllheli.

Nearby

Pwllheli is a bustling sea- and fishing-port and a popular tourist centre. Once famous for its oyster and lobster fisheries, it is probably now more well known for the large Butlin's holiday camp situated nearby.

A little further along the coast is Abersoch, a well known sailing and seaside centre and beyond, on a west-facing coast, is Hell's Mouth, the scene of many a shipwreck.

Ride 7

To the Summit of Snowdon

An energetic circular route from Llanberis to the summit of Snowdon returning by descending on the Snowdon Ranger Path to Llyn Cwellyn and a road route back to the starting point.

Maps: Landranger 1:50,000 series. Sheet number 115

Distance: 20½ miles (33 km)

Waymarked: The bridleways are very clearly marked

Gradients: The summit of Snowdon is 3560 feet (1085 metres) above sea level. On the ascent up the Llanberis path, the first part of the climb is up a steep tarmac track. This is the steepest part of the whole ascent, except for the final yards to the summit. Once you come off the tarmac section, the gradient is very much easier. On the descent, the steepest parts are at the top.

Surface: The bridleways are potentially very slippery when wet and there is a fair amount of loose stone. This is strictly a ride for mountain bicycles. If you are in any doubt, get off and walk for a while.

Future Proposals: N/A

Other Cycle Routes Linking: Rides in Beddgelert forest are nearby

Bicycle Hire: Llanberis

Shops and Refreshments: Llanberis, Snowdon and various villages on the return route. It is wise to take basic provisions

Special Comments: Do not forget your camera

Special Warnings: Heed advice offered by rangers, walkers and cyclists who are descending towards you. Tell somebody where you are going (if alone, phone a friend and arrange to phone again when you return in the evening). There are plenty of safety warnings and much information on good mountain practice, most of which is good common sense. Try to imagine that you have strayed from the main path and fallen off your bicycle, incapacitating yourself in some way. What would you do to attract the attention of possible helpers and will you be missed later in the day? A couple of very simple but very good safety aids, if you are alone, are a whistle and a cheap thermal blanket.

Permits: By mutual agreement, cyclists are not allowed on the bridleways during the summer months between 1st June and the 30th of September after 10am and before 5.00pm. During the remaining daylight hours and from October to the end of May access is unrestricted.

Throughout the compilation of this guide one of the most desirable requisites in the creation of a good cycle route has been the avoidance of the 'heartbreak hill' syndrome. For this route, this requisite has had to be thrown out of the window. This is a circular route to and from the summit of the highest mountain in Wales. Do not be put off by the prospect, because it can be tackled by any reasonably healthy cyclist willing to have a go. You do not require super fitness for this ride, although a certain level of general good health is desirable. If you can walk around the shops for half a day without needing a week in bed to recover, you can cycle up Snowdon.

It is important to have the right equipment and if you are not entirely confident in your own bicycle, it may well be worth considering the hire of a machine from one of the local specialists. They know the conditions and thus will supply what you need. It is also good practice to wear a helmet. Particularly on rough or slippery descents make sure that you stay on the path at all times, to avoid any exciting surprises or unplanned descents. A few items which are worth carrying are a compass, a whistle, an Ordnance Survey map and some form of emergency protection such as a thermal blanket (these come folded to a tiny size, little larger than a spare inner tube).

The 'Snowdon Ranger' Youth Hostel welcomes cyclists

Snowdon is the highest mountain in Wales and southern Britain. An ascent and descent by bicycle is a satisfying and memorable experience, a fine achievement to enter into your life's log book. If you have a choice, pick a clear day because the views are stunning. Snow can be a problem in the winter months up until Easter and mist is more prevalent in the Spring than in the Summer and Autumn. A clear and crisp October day would be an ideal choice.

Access Points

There are several bridleway paths up (and down!) Snowdon and good information on other alternatives may be obtained from the tourist offices. This route goes up the Llanberis Path by the railway and descends via the Snowdon Ranger Path. This is not a random selection of routes but one that is chosen carefully as the easiest method of creating a round trip route. The Llanberis path would offer a slightly easier descent than the Snowdon Ranger Path and if you are not wanting to carry out the full round trip, an ascent and descent via this path would be a most satisfying achievement.

From the choices of routes available, this suggested circular tour presents a fine combination of relative ease, high excitement and good interest. This route is described with a starting point in Llanberis where there is good parking available.

The Route

1. From Llanberis turn off the A4086 by taking the road just south of the station Victoria Terrace (Rhes Fickoria).
2. Follow the Llanberis Bridleway for the summit. (**The first tarmac section is as steep as it gets.**)
3. All the way up, the little railway will be close at hand. Initially it will be on your right.
4. About half way up you will cross the railway to leave it on your left.
5. About three-quarters of the way up, you will cross the railway again.
6. Upon reaching the summit, retrace your route back to point where you passed the Snowdon Ranger Bridleway.

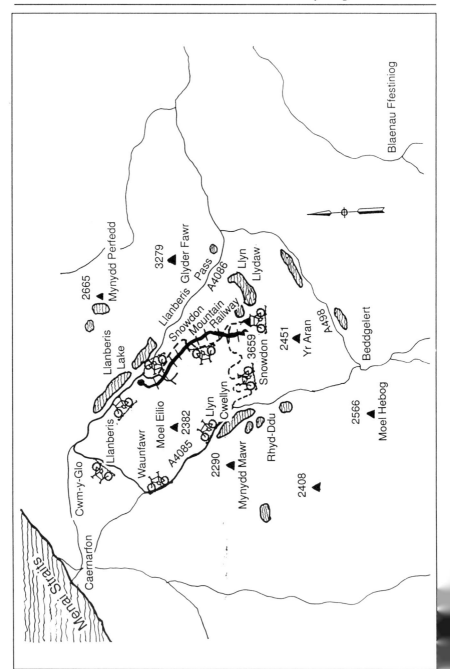

7. Turn left and follow this bridleway, with great care, to the bottom by Llyn Cwellyn and the Youth Hostel.

8. Turn right along the A4085 and follow the road with the lake on your left. Continue straight through the village of Betws Garmon and to the village of Waunfawr, where you should turn right signed to Ceunant.

9. Follow the minor road out through Croesywaun going straight on at the four way cross roads towards the Ceunant and the A4086.

10. After passing through Ceunant, cross the A4086 towards Pont Rhythallt.

11. At the T-junction, bear right to cross Afon Rhythallt and turn right at the next junction signed to Penisa Waun.

12. At the junction with the B4547, turn right and re-cross the river to the lake side road (A4086) turning left to follow it back to return to Llanberis.

Nearby

The Snowdon Mountain Railway has a gauge of 2 foot $7\frac{1}{2}$ inches. It runs for a distance of over $4\frac{1}{2}$ miles and climbs 3,086 feet from 353 feet above sea level in Llanberis to 3,439 feet at the summit. The easiest gradient is 1 in 50 for the first 350 yard stretch and the steepest is 1 in $5\frac{1}{2}$.

The railway was built between 1894 and 1896 after an initiative by the directors of the London and North-Western Railway Company who had built a branch line from Caernarvon to Llanberis in 1869. The local landowner had taken some convincing but had finally been persuaded by his daughter Enid and a promise of the Chairmanship of the company.

On the inaugural trip disaster struck when the No 1 locomotive, Ladas, derailed and plunged down the mountain. A full year was to pass before the directors were satisfied that modifications had made the line safe and the second trip was headed by the locomotive *Enid*, named after the chairman's daughter.

Ride 8

Forestry Tracks in Beddgelert Forest, at the Foot of Snowdon

Extremely pleasant forestry riding little used forestry tracks and bridleways in the Llyn Cwellyn valley at the foot of mighty Snowdon.

Maps: Landranger 1:50,000 series. Sheet number 115

Distance: 6 miles (9.5 km)

Waymarked: No, but the forestry tracks are clear to see

Gradients: Plenty of climbs available but stick to the contour tracks if you prefer where the gradients are fairly easy.

Surface: Stick to the well-surfaced forestry vehicle tracks. These are used by heavy machines and offer generally good surface conditions.

Future Proposals: N/A

Other Cycle Routes Linking: Nearby routes from Beddgelert and to the summit of Snowdon

Bicycle Hire: Beddgelert

Shops and Refreshments: Beddgelert, take some supplies with you

Special Comments: N/A

Special Warnings: N/A

Permits: N/A

There are several extremely pleasant rides through the forest. There are easily-found loops which are ideal for timed fitness exercises or for short introductory family rides away from traffic. These delightful tracks take you through a wonderful forest at the foot of the mighty ever-present Snowdon. Ride through lush glades and nursery plantations of freshly-planted conifers and enjoy the magical peace of Llyn Cwellyn, all within a short distance from a convenient car park. This can form a short ride or can be made into a full day's exploration, as there are plenty of tracks to use. Perhaps this is an ideal venue to simply go and 'play' with your bicycles and can be a good-practice ground before attempting the ascent of Snowdon.

For fitness purposes, there is enough gradient to be suitable for personal training by riding against your own time targets. To make the best out of time training, set yourself an easy benchmark time by riding a route once at a normal, fairly leisurely pace. Try to improve your time by a small margin on each subsequent run. Do not make the mistake of setting out at a blistering pace and subsequently attempting to better your lap. This will do little for long term fitness and muscular strain can put your short-term fitness in jeopardy.

The dominant trees within Beddgelert are douglas fir, european larch, and norway spruce. The bird life of the forest includes heron, kingfisher, and dippers around Llyn Cwellyn. This is an ideal location for family groups and the perfect spot to introduce newcomers to a taste of the delights of forestry cycling.

Access Points

Start your rides from the car park off the A4085, north-west of Beddgelert. The forest is then on your left.

A picnic spot in the forest near Beddgelert

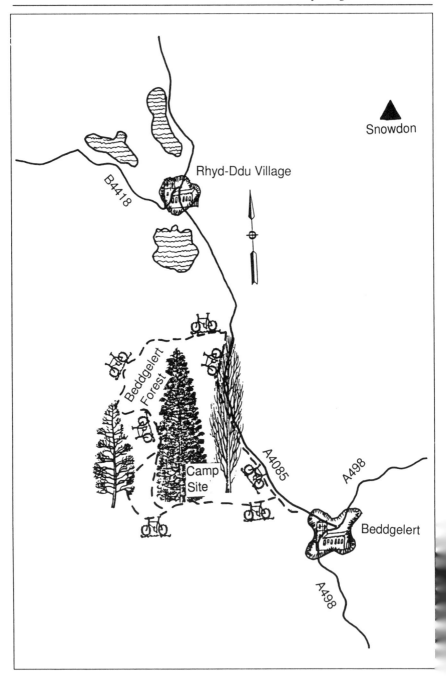

The Route

1. Leave the 4085 by turning left at the point where the forest is signed north-west of Beddgelert, where there is a good car park.

2. Alternatively, from Beddgelert, turn left into the forest on the edge of the town off the A4085. For a very short distance you will follow a tarmac road, which is only used occasionally by motor vehicles for access.

3. Cross over the rushing waters of Nant Colwyn, which will never be far away from the contour track. It is well worth stopping here just to enjoy the beauty of the water and the wild flowers in the lush base of the stream valley. Keep still for long enough and you are quite likely to see examples of some of the creatures who live by the water here.

4. After about four hundred meters uphill you should take the track on your right. This will loosely follow the contour into Beddgelert Forest. Once in the forest there is a choice of well-surfaced forestry tracks all of which are open to cyclists. The choice is yours; some tracks climb into the high ground to the west while others keep close to convenient contours.

Nearby

Beddgelert is a lovely spot to visit, the confluence of two rock strewn rivers, tumbling down from their deep mountain valley passes (see ride 9).

On the western side of Beddgelert stands Moel Hebog (the Hill of the Hawk). The ascent to 2,566 feet is one of the most popular climbs from the town. It takes about two hours going up and typically an hour descending and is therefore ideal for a half-day expedition. To climb Moel Hebog, find the track on the north side of the Goat Hotel.

Ride 9

The Valleys of Beddgelert

A fairly energetic ride which takes you high above the hauntingly beautiful valleys around Beddgelert and returns you to the starting point past the gentle waters of Llyn Dinas.

Maps: Landranger 1:50,000 series. Sheet numbers 115

Distance: 10½ miles (17 km)

Waymarked: No

Gradients: An energetic ride with some steep climbing and equally breathtaking descents

Surface: Tarmac

Future Proposals: N/A

Other Cycle Routes Linking: N/A

Bicycle Hire: Beddgelert

Shops and Refreshments: Beddgelert and clear mountain water, otherwise take provisions

Special Comments: Parts of this ride use stretches of 'A' road, where you are bound to encounter a certain amount of traffic. The traffic is however, normally quite slow moving and the use of these roads is justified by the topography and the great natural beauty of the valley passes, which would be missed if the 'A' roads were not used.

Special Warnings: N/A

Permits: N/A

If Beddgelert were a book it would be on every well-stocked shelf in the land. The sheer magic of the mountain passes that approach the town are the key to its fascination but the town itself has a special charm, centred on the confluence of wild rocky rivers as they tumble down from the higher grounds of Snowdonia to meet in a torrent of confusion and whirling eddies.

The name of the town is well-entrenched in folklore (see ride 8) and there are many interesting sites to make exploration worthwhile. There is a disused railway footpath leading along the Pass of Aberglaslyn, south of the town which makes an excellent walk for anybody not taking part in the cycling.

The ride follows through this pass before climbing into the high ground to the west of the town and subsequently descending to Llyn Dinas and returning past Sygun Copper Mining Museum to Beddgelert. Allow yourself plenty of time (at least half a day) to give yourself a good chance to really appreciate the superb landscapes and scenic views along the route.

Above Beddgelert

Access Points

Beddgelert is situated approximately ten miles to the north of Porthmadog and is approached via the A498. The drive inland from the coast is a pleasure in its own right.

The Route

1. From the main car park in Beddgelert, (by the Royal Goat Hotel), turn right onto the A498, to pass the Royal Goat Hotel on the right.

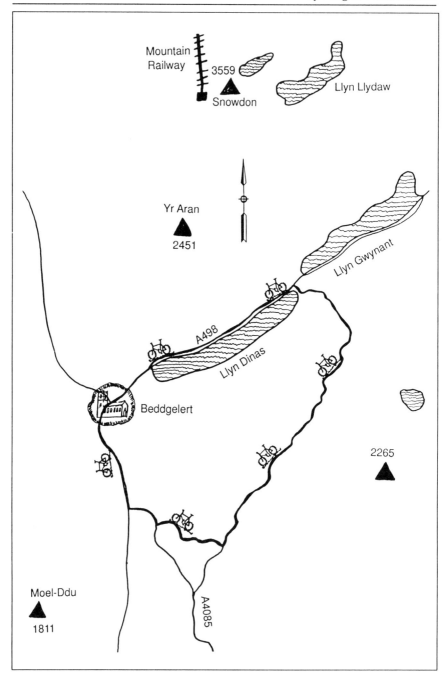

2. After passing out of Beddgelert and through the Pass of Aberglaslyn,.

3. Cross Pont Aberglaslyn, the bridge across the rocky river onto the A4085, signed to Penrhyndeudraeth, Maentwrog and Dolgellau.

4. After a short distance, take the minor road up to the left signed to Nantmor.

5. Climb up the narrow single track road and carry straight on through the village of Nantmor.

6. At the T-junction, turn left.

7. Follow this road, which has a number of gates, to the junction with the A498 at the head of Llyn Dinas.

8. Turn left along the A498 to pass the Sygun Copper Mining Museum and return to Beddgelert.

9. Turn left across the bridge in Beddgelert to return to the car park.

Nearby

As legend will have us believe, Beddgelert translates to 'Grave of Gelert'. Gelert was a dog, the hound of Llewellyn whose grave is marked by a few stones. The date of death is said to have been 1205. Having been left in charge of Llewellyn's infant child, Gelert defended the child by killing a wolf. Prince Llewellyn, returning to find the cot overturned and the room sprinkled in blood, immediately assumed that Gelert was the culprit and killed him with a single slash of his sword. Moments later, but too late for poor old Gelert, Llewellyn found his child safe and unharmed under the cot and then the bloody body of the big bad wolf.

Historical research has demonstrated that this story was invented by David Prichard, an 18th century innkeeper and subsequently adopted by a contemporary ballad singer from where it entered into the vague mid-world of legend and myth. It was in this manner therefore, that David Prichard inadvertently invented one of the finest manufactured tourist attractions that North Wales has ever known. To this day thousands of people flock every year to visit 'Gelert's Grave'.

Ride 10
Great Orme's Head and Llandudno

A great coastal ride around the stunning rocky coastline of Great Orme's Head, based on the elegant traditional resort of Llandudno.

Maps: Landranger 1:50,000 series. Sheet number 115

Distance: 7½ miles (12 km)

Waymarked: No

Gradients: A few little climbs but nothing too serious and some pleasant freewheeling descents

Surface: Tarmac

Future Proposals: N/A

Other Cycle Routes Linking: N/A

Bicycle Hire: Llandudno

Shops and Refreshments: Plenty in Llandudno and around Great Orme's Head

Special Comments: N/A

Special Warnings: This is an exposed costal road and can be quite windy

Permits: The road around Great Orme's Head is a toll road but is free to cyclists

---

The elegant town of Llandudno, situated on the level neck of a promontory between the Great and Little Orme's Heads, is the largest resort town in Wales. It has retained its charm while moving with the inevitable non-stop march of progress and boasts a range of facilities and shops to compete with any major metropolis. Most major stores and banks are represented as well as plenty of smaller interesting shops. The North shore crescent shaped beach is renowned to be the finest for bathing in the area with firm sand and quiet waters and there is a glorious promenade, well-sheltered from the prevailing westerly winds.

The ride around the town and the base of Great Orme's Head is effectively a tour of the resort and its direct surroundings and includes some of the finest coastal scenery in the whole of Wales. Great Orme's Head rises 679 feet out of the sea and, although it is not on the intended route of this ride, it can be ascended by bicycle from the coastal road. There are three easier ways to get to the top of Great Orme's Head, by automobile, by a funicular tramway or by a cable car. Alternatively, an ascent on foot will allow you to pass through the 'Happy Valley', an ornate garden with a fantastic profusion of plants.

This popular cycle ride is ideal for a couple of hours' exercise while enjoying some of the finest coastal scenery in Britain. The historical aspect of Llandudno, as one of the earliest tourist towns of the railway age, is interesting. The tourist information office has some interesting information on the subject of the old-established attractions of Llandudno and is well worth a visit.

Access Points

The route directions are given with a starting point at the promenade information centre. It is important to go around Great Orme's Head in the right direction (anti-clockwise) because of the one-way traffic rules.

Rounding Great Orme's Head

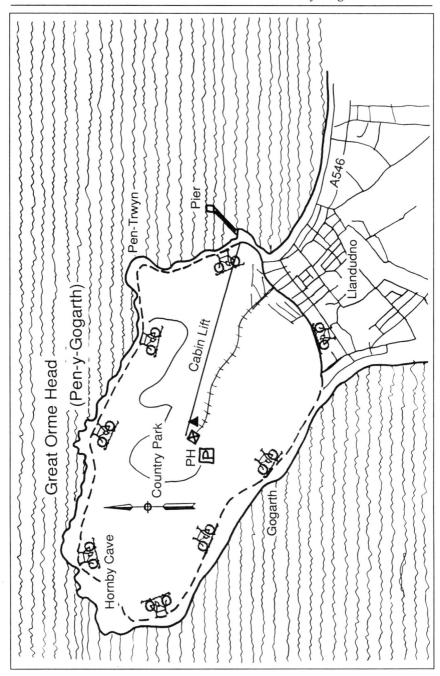

Great Orme Head
(Pen-y-Gogarth)

Pen-Trwyn

Pier

A546

Llandudno

Cabin Lift

Country Park

PH

Hornby Cave

Gogarth

The Route

1. From the promenade information centre head north-west towards Great Orme's Head with the sea on your right.

2. At the toll office (no charge for bicycles) carry straight on, keeping the sea on your right.

3. After rounding Great Orme's Head, keep left to pass the Gardens and the entrance to the funicular railway.

4. Go right along the promenade to return to your starting point.

Nearby

Little Orme's Head: As its name suggests, Little Orme's Head, at 465 feet, is not as large as its big brother but it is well worth a visit. The cliffs are more craggy and there are some good views. The Lewis Carroll memorial (of Alice in Wonderland fame) on the west shore is to commemorate the fact that he stayed in town with Dean Liddell and his family, particularly his daughter Alice Liddell, who inspired 'Alice in Wonderland'.

Great Orme's Head: An ascent of Great Orme's Head is essential, many visitors try more than one way to the top. Probably the most exciting way to descend Great Orme's Head is by toboggan on the purpose-built run.

The Marine Drive Project: This was completed in 1879 and the initial cost was £14,000. It remained in private ownership until the Urban District Council purchased it in 1897. In 1910, they abolished the toll for pedestrians (and cyclists).

Ride 11

Conwy Castle

*A ride out into the country lanes and valleys south of Conwy and a
look at the famous castle, town walls and Conwy bridges.*

Maps: Landranger 1:50,000 series. Sheet numbers 115

Distance: 10½ miles (17 km)

Waymarked: No, a rural ride with good signposts

Gradients: One or two slight climbs but not enough to ruin your day

Surface: Tarmac

Future Proposals: N/A

Other Cycle Routes Linking: N/A

Bicycle Hire: Conwy

Shops and Refreshments: Conwy and several villages mentioned along the route

Special Comments: N/A

Special Warnings: N/A

Permits: N/A

Conwy is a lovely old town, unmistakable for its town walls, its
Castle and Telford's beautiful suspension bridge. The town has a
superb coastal location and is historically a major road and rail
staging post along the main artery route from Liverpool to Ireland
via Holyhead. If you have time, take a walk along the castle 15-foot-
thick walls. This half mile length of wall is laid out in the shape of
a Welsh harp! There are eight drum towers and no less than 21
charming semi circular towers spaced evenly along the length of the
walls.

There are three major bridge crossings in Conwy. As well as
Telford's suspension bridge, there is a tubular bridge, the work of
Robert Stephenson in 1848, and a graceful modern road bridge
which was completed in 1958. The main trunk road now bypasses
the town and crosses the river through a tunnel.

Conwy Castle

This ride takes you south from Conwy through some delightful valley and rural lane scenery. It is not too energetic although there are a few slight climbs. There is plenty of peaceful countryside to enjoy along the way and the village of Roewen is a good half way stopping off point.

Access Points

The starting point of the ride is from the western/castle end of the old Conwy suspension bridge. There are plenty of good car parks in Conwy. The directions are given in an anti-clockwise direction to avoid as many right-hand turns as possible.

The Route

1. From the western/castle end of Conwy suspension bridge, with your back to the bridge, make your way to the road and turn left up towards the mini island.

2. Turn left at the mini-island by the tourist information office

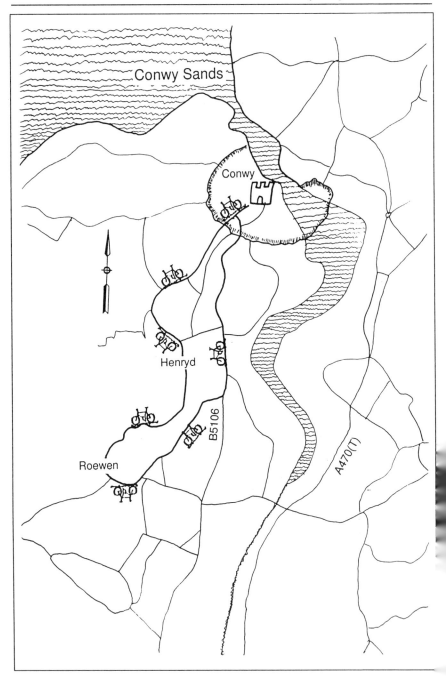

signed to Trefriw. Under the arches, follow the road (B5106) as it bends to the right.

3. Where the B5106 bends sharp left, turn right signed to Sychnant. After a short distance, turn left into Hendre Road.

4. At the crossroads, carry straight on.

5. Take the left-hand turn signed to Roewen and Hendre.

6. At the T-junction, with a signpost to Hendre to the left, turn right.

7. At the next left-hand junction turn left, signed to Roewen.

8. Just after a post box and just before a stone bridge, turn right down a narrow lane. After a short distance you will pass the Gwern Borter manor.

9. At the T-junction, at the end of this lane, turn left.

10. Follow down the short hill into Roewen and turn left at the T-junction.

11. Turn left again at the second T-junction and continue through the village.

12. After some distance, turn left onto the B5106 and following this road for a distance, rejoin the outward route as you pass into the suburbs of Conwy at the aforementioned sharp bend (which is now a right-hand bend).

Nearby

Conwy suspension bridge was built by Thomas Telford in 1826. In its day it was a very major improvement of the main Liverpool to Holyhead and Ireland trunk road. Two major bottlenecks along this route had been the river crossing at Conwy and the Menai Straits to Anglesey. Telford's task was to bridge these two obstructions, hence the obvious similarity of style between the Conwy and Menai Bridges. The towers of Conwy Bridge were designed to blend in with the medieval turrets of Conwy Castle and the resulting architecture is therefore a pleasing and rare close mix of folly copy and original.

Ride 12

Gwydyr Forest, Betws-y-Coed

*Superb waymarked cycle tracks in the magnificent Gwydyr Forest
centred on Y Stablau (The Stables) Snowdonia National Park
information centre in the centre of Betws-y-Coed*

Maps: Landranger 1:50,000 series. Sheet number 115

Distance: 6 or 9 miles. (9.5 or 14.5 km)

Waymarked: Yellow boards with a black bicycle symbol

Gradients: The waymarked routes are well thought out and avoid any serious gradients. This has created a facility suitable for the family and beginner (if you take your time) while maintaining enough interest for the serious mountain biker.

Surface: Forestry tracks. Well-drained consolidated surfaces.

Future Proposals: Constant maintenance and improvement where possible

Other Cycle Routes Linking: N/A

Bicycle Hire: Beics Bettws (behind Tan Lan Restaurant)

Shops and Refreshments: Plenty of choice in Betws y Coed

Special Comments: If you are planning some serious rough riding, wear a helmet

Special Warnings: Slippery when wet

Permits: N/A

Gwydyr Forest, situated around Betws-y-Coed, south of Conwy via the A470 is one of the finest forests in this delightful region. Although Betws-y-Coed is on the mainstream tourist route Gwydyr is well away from the main thoroughfares, and is often ignored by the casual traveller, who is traditionally more intent on admiring the countryside from the roads or little railway routes while exploring the whole Snowdonia region. The forest offers some superb cycling for the dedicated mountain biker or for the family group, all in absolutely magnificent wild and unspoilt surroundings.

Betws-y-Coed, roughly translated from the ancient Welsh as 'Sanctuary in the Wood', is sited at the confluence of the softly flowing Conwy River with the more excitable Llugwy and Lledr

Rivers. The Swallow falls, situated $2\frac{1}{2}$ miles to the west of the town off the Capel Curig road, are a fine and refreshing sight. On the River Conwy, two miles to the south on the Pentrefoelas Road are the Conwy Falls and the magical Fairy Glen.

The forest itself is planted amidst rolling countryside and has elevations ranging between 500 and 1000 feet (150 and 300 metres) above sea level. The waymarked route is well thought out and follows the contour hugging forestry tracks. This is a fine ride with plenty of spots to sit and simply enjoy the true beauty of the forest and the splendour of the wildlife. Look carefully and you may see deer, hawks, squirrels and hares.

Access Points

The waymarked tracks can be accessed from the centre of Betws-y-Coed. Information is available from Y Stablau (The Stables) Snowdonia National Park information centre. There is good car parking adjacent to the centre. To find the waymarked routes, turn right out of the car park along the A5(T).

Gwydyr Forest

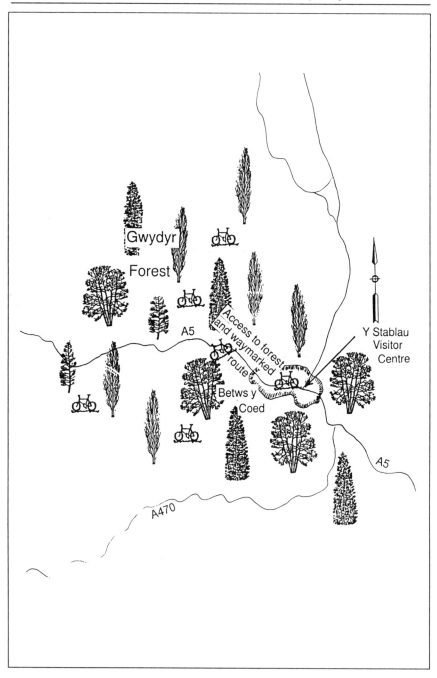

You will see the beginning of the forest tracks on your left just as you begin to leave Betws-y-Coed by the speed derestriction signs. Turn left up a road marked 'unsuitable for motor vehicles.' The bicycle access climbs up from the beginning of this road and is clearly marked with a forestry 'waymark' notice.

The Route

The waymarked route sets out from the edge of Betws-y-Coed. A choice of 6 miles or 9 miles is available and is clearly marked as you follow the waymarks. Good interpretive information is available from Y Stablau in the town. Excursions from the main route are quite acceptable as long as you keep to official forestry tracks and cause no damage. Bear in mind that unless you are properly equipped and have some experience or guidance, you are well advised to keep to the official routes.

Nearby

Betws-y-Coed has long been a favourite haunt of landscape artists. Although it is surrounded by mountainous country, the town itself is a mere 80 feet above sea level and famed for its good air and light quality. The rich soils encourage a wide range of plant growth creating a rich and diverse show of colour all year round. It is also a favourite anglers retreat, not so surprising with the choice of waters in the surrounding hills and valleys. In 1847, the celebrated landscape painter, David Cox, painted a new signboard for his favourite hostelry, the Royal Oak Hotel. The board is still at the hotel today, albeit in a glass case for posterity.

Ride 13

Clocaenog Forest

A fine ride in one of the great forests of north-east Wales amid a magnificent and unspoilt natural landscape.

Maps: Landranger 1:50,000 series. Sheet number 116

Distance: 15 miles (24 km)

Waymarked: Latest information and maps available at the Llyn Brenig Visitor Centre off the B4501. Other information available from the Bod Petrual Forest Visitor Centre off the B5105

Gradients: A few ups and downs

Surface: Well drained and solid forestry and minor roads

Future Proposals: N/A

Other Cycle Routes Linking: N/A

Bicycle Hire: At Llyn Brenig mountain bike centre

Shops and Refreshments: At the Llyn Brenig Forest Visitor Centre off the B5105)

Special Comments: N/A

Special Warnings: If you decide to try the rough mountain biking tracks (away from the wide vehicular forest tracks), make sure you wear a helmet and expect a few falls

Permits: N/A

The Clocaenog forest provides good traffic free family rides on forestry tracks or, if you prefer, a good selection of rough riding for the dedicated mountain biker. Set in the splendour of north-east Wales the forest is is an idyllic spot with beautiful mature trees, bubbling watercourses and a fantastic array of wild flower and plant life. Reached by car on the B5105 7 miles south-west of Ruthin and Denbigh, or by Llyn Brenig visitor centre off the B4501, the forest is now well into its second rotation and boasts a great variety of tree species including large areas of mature broad leaved woodland.

The dominant trees within Clocaenog are tall douglas fir, which can reach heights of over 130 feet ($39\frac{1}{2}$ metres), hardy european larch, elegant norway spruce (real Christmas trees, but most are far too big for your hallway). Other species include ash and cypress while some examples of birch and oak are making ground in the clearings. Around parts of the perimeter are mature oak, ash and hawthorn which generally pre-date the managed forest.

The bird life of the forest includes heron, kingfisher, and dippers around the Brenig Reservoir as well as chiff chaff, tree creepers and wood pigeons in the woods. As well as the cycle-friendly forestry roads, there is a range of lovely waymarked walks and the free-to-enter Bod Petrual Forest Visitor Centre, where there is a first class presentation of a 'past and present' forest story, told in pictures and dioramas.

Access Points

Clocaenog Forest can be approached from the B5105 Cerrigydrudion to Ruthin road. This ride is described from the Llyn Brenig Visitor Centre off the B4501.There is good car parking and bicycle hire available from here.

The Route

There are several choices of routes available in the forest. This route has been chosen because it gives access to the network maze of forestry roads and will give a good impression of the sort of riding available in the forest.

1. From the Llyn Brenig Visitor Centre follow the one way system of the tarmac service road, heading north with the reservoir to your right.

2. At the first Exit junction, keep right to follow the signs for the nature trail and water sports centre.

3. After passing the water sports and mountain bike centre, you will arrive at the B4501.

4. Go straight over the B4501 and follow the fine forest trail.

5. At the T-junction of forestry tracks turn around to return to the visitor centre or turn left or right to explore the forest. A left turn will eventually lead towards the Alwen Reservoir.

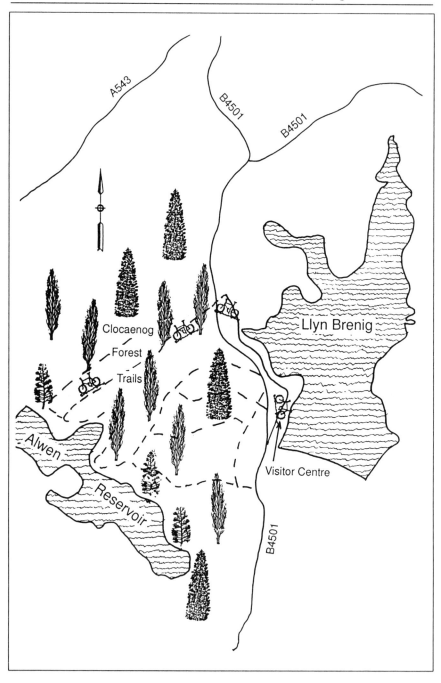

Note. From the Bod Petrual Visitor Centre, there are forestry roads and tracks leading through the forest in various directions. A very pleasant and easy route is north of the centre through the forest to Llyn Brenig. You will never be far from the river courses and their little tributaries which form a narrow vale through the heart of the forest and it is a delight to see the crystal clear water flowing confidently across the rock strewn stream bed. Have a rest on one of the lovely mossy shaded banks and look up through the tree canopy while you listen to the constant babbling of the water.

The best rough mountain biking area is from the Bod Petrual Visitor Centre. Details are available at the centre.

Nearby

Along your chosen route, look out for birds, wild life and the masses of wild flowers in the undergrowth and hedges. In springtime primroses and violets will be in bloom while later on in the year foxgloves and campions will provide plentiful colour. Follow the valley back to where you started. See how you feel and perhaps go out and do it again.

Ride 14

Denbigh Castle

A most pleasant simple and short rural circular from Denbigh Castle. An ideal family trip.

Maps: Landranger 1:50,000 series. Sheet number 116

Distance: 7½ miles (12 km)

Waymarked: No

Gradients: A slight climb to return to the castle

Surface: Tarmac country lane

Future Proposals: None

Other Cycle Routes Linking: No

Bicycle Hire: Denbigh

Shops and Refreshments: Denbigh

Special Comments: N/A

Special Warnings: N/A

Permits: N/A

Denbigh is a pleasant and ancient market town with a superb ruined castle. The town is sited on a high promontory of ground and enjoys excellent views over the surrounding countryside. It is a very popular centre for touring and well known for its fishing facilities.

This is an easy ride, ideal for a family group. It follows very quiet country lanes to the south of the town. For a great half day out, cycling just for the sheer hell of it and exploring a lovely region of countryside, this is an ideal route and there are plenty of points of interest along the way.

This area is a rich agricultural region with good soils owing their origins to the rivers running down from the Clocaenog Forest area. The earliest references to farming activities date back to the 13th century.

Access Points

The starting point of the ride is from the castle car park, Denbigh.
You could start from anywhere along the route, the junction of the
A543 and the A525 on the edge of the town being a good alternative.
The directions use quiet country lanes wherever possible to avoid
traffic.

At Denbigh Castle, high above the town

The Route

1. From the car park of Denbigh Castle, go via the grasscrete drive
    past the old tower on the right to the tarmac public road.

2. Turn right and follow the one way system downhill via Lon Parc
    (Park Street) towards the bottom of the town.

3. At the T-junction at the bottom of the hill, turn right.

4. At the road island junction of the A543 and the A525, go straight
    ahead, signed to Ruthin along the A525.

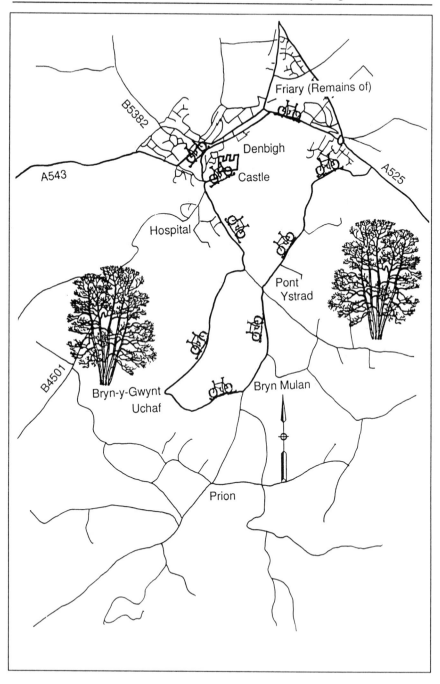

Friary (Remains of)

B5382

A543

Denbigh
Castle

A525

Hospital

Pont
Ystrad

B4501

Bryn-y-Gwynt
Uchaf

Bryn Mulan

Prion

5. After only a very short distance, past the speed derestriction signs, turn right up the minor lane signed to Brookhouse.

6. At the T-junction, turn left.

7. Go over an old stone bridge and follow the road around to the left signed to Glyn and Llanrhaeadr, i.e. taking the left turn at the staggered crossroads.

8. Turn right at the next junction signed to Prion.

9. Keep right at the next junction following the Prion sign.

10. At the next give way junction by the letter box, go left signed to Prion and Saron.

11. After about a ¼ of a mile take the right fork at the Y-junction.

12. At the T-junction after a couple of miles, turn left, signed to Denbigh.

13. At the next T-junction, turn right, signed to Denbigh.

14. After a short distance, turn right signed to the Castle.

15. Follow this road back to the car park.

Nearby

Denbigh Castle was originally built by the Earl of Lincoln in 1282 and stands on a 467 foot hillock. The substantial ruins include eight magnificent towers and the main gatehouse. Other nearby ruins include Leicester's Folly, which is part of an unfinished church, and the old Denbigh town wall. Just under the castle walls is the site of a cottage which was once home to H M Stanley, the great African Explorer of Dr Livingstone fame. The town's museum is well worth a visit and other very old buildings which are of interest include the 16th-century town hall and the 17th-century Bull Inn.

Ride 15

Ruabon Mountain and the Lead Mines of Coedpoeth

A superbly spectacular ride around Ruabon Mountain, the Eglwyseg Mountain and Esclusham Mountain, with great ridge views over the Vale of Llangollen.

Maps: Landranger 1:50,000 series. Sheet numbers 117

Distance: 22½ miles (36 km)

Waymarked: No. Keep turning left at every opportunity

Gradients: Not as much as one might imagine but there are inevitably some hill climbs. Mostly short and sharp

Surface: Tarmac country lane and mountain road

Future Proposals: N/A

Other Cycle Routes Linking: No

Bicycle Hire: Wrexham

Shops and Refreshments: Best to take some supplies with you

Special Comments: N/A

Special Warnings: N/A

Permits: N/A

This superb tour of the Ruabon Mountain, the Eglwyseg Mountain and the Esclusham Mountain from Coedpoeth, west of Wrexham, and north-west of Llangollen, traces a route via very quiet mountain roads and little rural lanes to form a magnificent circular trip from the fascinating Minera Lead Mining complex. These are some of the finest of all of the Welsh Mountains and the scenery is spectacular but the area is perhaps not so well known as other parts of North Wales.

Although it may seem difficult to believe today, the area was once a busy industrial mining centre with great reserves of lead, silver and zinc in the mines which extended under the mountains. The earliest references to these mining activities date back to the 13th century. The mines came to an eventual halt for economic reasons with decline of reserves and stiff foreign competition being the cited causes.

This is a fairly energetic ride with several sharp climbs but the views and the general scenery offer ample reward for your efforts. Treat this as a leisurely day trip, take supplies with you and you will have a wonderful day's cycling.

Access Points

Approach the Lead Mining Museum and country park off the B4526 in Coedpoeth by taking the B4526 off the A525. In Coedpoeth, by the Five Crosses Industrial Estate on the A525, turn left and the B4526 turning will be found signed to Minera Mwynglawdd and Lead Mines shortly on the right-hand side.

The Route

1. From the car park of the Minera Lead Mines mining museum and country park, turn left onto the B5426 signed to Minera.

2. After a short distance turn left into the minor road signed to World's End.

3. Follow this road over the open mountain and descend through woodland and lush valleys, keeping to the same road.

4. Go left at the Eglwyseg T-junction signed to Llangollen.

5. At the next junction keep left and at the following junction keep left signed to 'Panorama'.

6. Continue straight ahead onto the open mountain road with superb views to the right over the Vale of Llangollen.

7. Keep left at the Y-junction keeping the high road.

8. To return to the Lead Mines car park from here, simply keep left at every possible opportunity. Be careful not to turn along private drives or no-through-roads, but apart from that take every left turn and you will return to the starting point.

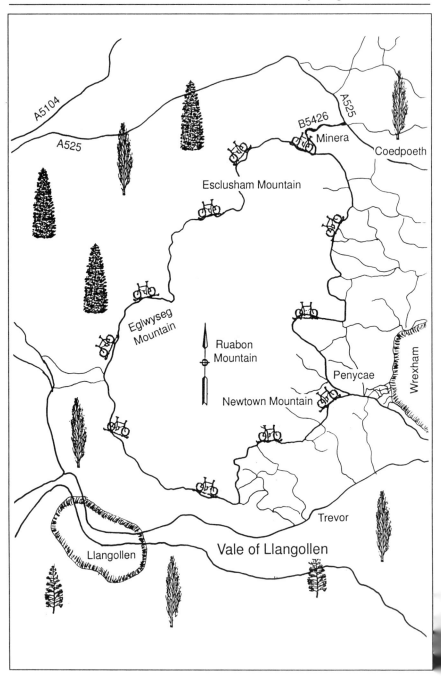

(If you do inadvertently turn along a no-through-road, none go very far and you will soon discover the error. The route back is all tarmac surface).

Nearby

Minera Lead Mines (Pyllau Plwm Mwynglawdd) Mining Museum in the Dyffryn Clywedog Valley is an interesting exhibition of the lead and zinc mining industry of the area. The mine retains a great deal of its original industrial archeology and has a working water wheel and machinery, which can be viewed in a superb walk-around demonstration whereby the visitor can appreciate what actually happened. There are good interpretative information stands as well as an excellent indoor exhibition and a discovery trail which makes a pleasant walk around the immediate area.

Ride 16

The Llangollen Canal

Siambr Wen Bridge Llangollen (Number 45) over the Pont-cysyllte Aqueduct to Irish Bridge (Number 27). A fascinating, traffic-free ride along the historic towpath of the Llangollen Canal.

Maps: 1:50,000 map series, sheet numbers: 126

Distance: 11 miles (17.5 km)

Waymarked: Just follow the waterway. Most bridges are numbered or named (see map)

Gradients: None

Surface: Solid and well-drained natural surface. Some sections can be slippery when wet

Future Proposals: British Waterways is committed to maintaining or improving the towpath

Other Cycle Routes Linking: There are other sections of the Llangollen Canal where cycling is permitted. Refer to the Canal Manager's office for details

Bicycle Hire: Llangollen

Shops and Refreshments: Llangollen, Ruabon, Froncysyllte

Special Comments: N/A

Special Warnings: Beware of slippery surfaces and potholes. Beware of mooring ropes, anglers' equipment, bollards and mooring stakes. Dismount when passing under bridge holes. Dismount and push over the Pont-cysyllte Aqueduct. Keep your speed down. A mistake on a narrow sections of towpath can end in a soaking.

Permits: A British Waterways permit is required for this ride. The permits are readily available by calling into a local British Waterways office or by writing to:The Canal Manager, British Waterways, Canal Office, Birch Road, Ellesmere, Shropshire SY12 9AA. The permits are free of charge.

This is a delightfully easy and rewarding ride, ideal for a family day out. It follows the towpath of the beautiful Llangollen Canal from Llangollen, past the villages of Trevor and Ruabon, over the 100C foot Pont-cysyllte Aqueduct, 120 feet over the River Dee (You mus dismount and push here) past the village of Froncysyllte to the poin where the canal is crossed by a feeder road between the A5(T) and the A483(T).

Cycling along a canal towpath is a real pleasure. There are no hills to impede your progress, the surface is good and as well as good views over the distant mountains, there is always the delight of the waterway with its profusion of plant and wildlife to keep you company.

The Llangollen Canal was built between 1796 and 1806 under the direction of the celebrated engineer, William Jessop. It was part of grand scheme of canals which were to serve the Mersey and the Severn via the Shropshire Union and, in the case of the Llangollen Canal, the coal and iron fields around Ruabon. The canal is one of the busiest cruising leisure waterways in Britain and is notable for the two great aqueducts at Pont-cysyllte and Chirk.

Crossing the Pontcycyllte aqueduct

Access Points

To access the canal from Llangollen town centre, cross the bridge

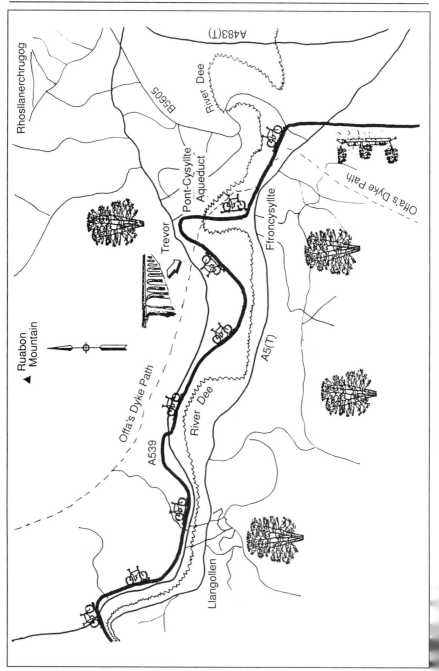

by the Royal Hotel and carry straight on up Wharf Hill. At bridge 27 use the feeder road between the A5(T) and the A483(T), approximately a mile east of Froncysyllte.

The Route

1. Join the canal towpath in Llangollen and turn right along the towpath to head in a south-easterly direction.
2. Continue along the towpath, crossing the canal at bridge 31 and then the Pont-cysyllte Aqueduct. Continue to Bridge 27 before turning to retrace the route.
3. After passing over the Pont-cysyllte Aqueduct, pass through the boat yard, go over the bridge and left to rejoin the canal a few yards further on.

Refreshments or shops can be accessed from bridge 41, bridge 29, and bridge 28.

Nearby

The Pont-cysyllte Aqueduct is considered to be one of the great wonders of the canal age. The picture, looking up from the River Dee Valley, is arguably the most famous image of the whole British canal system. Although the main canal engineer was William Jessop, the Pont-cysyllte Aqueduct is the work of Thomas Telford. When it was built, the design of the iron troughs linked together and set atop high stone piers was entirely untried and its proposal was treated with almost universal scepticism until it was built and proven. It took ten years to build and opened in 1805, to the amazement of the local people who were the first in the world to see boats being hauled across the sky by horses a hundred and twenty feet over their heads. In its day, this was truly a wonder of the world.

Llangollen is famous for its International Eisteddfod of music every July. If you have an ear for music and a liking for dance from all corners of the world, this is the place to be.

Ride 17

The River Dee: Corwen to Llangollen and Return

A pleasant and undemanding return ride along the soft Dee valley under the great flanks of the Llantysilio Mountain to the north and the wild Berwyn Range to the south.

Maps: Landranger 1:50,000 series. Sheet numbers 125 and 117

Distance: 23 miles (37 km)

Waymarked: No

Gradients: Easy undulating road following the River Dee

Surface: Tarmac, mainly minor road

Future Proposals: N/A

Other Cycle Routes Linking: Llangollen Canal – Ride No 16

Bicycle Hire: Llangollen

Shops and Refreshments: Corwen and Llangollen, otherwise take some provisions

Special Comments: N/A

Special Warnings: If you visit Llangollen, beware of the traffic on the short 'A' road section

Permits: N/A

To be successful in the art of cycling in North Wales, it is wise to follow valleys and although this is not always practical, occasionally a valley is worth following, even if it is not going where you are going. If it is your intention to avoid any steep climbs and if you enjoy riverside scenery and steep sided valleys, this may well be the ride for you. This River Dee valley ride somehow brings all the right facets of leisure cycling together in just the right balance.

The Llantysilio Mountain flanks the north of the valley with a bold and imposing presence and the wild and wonderful Berwyn Range commands the ground in the south. The graceful River Dee flows across the green fields to your immediate south shielded from your view only by grand old broadleaf trees, while further to the south, the lush wooded valley sides present a great backcloth to the panorama.

The riding is not too energetic, the only climbs being brief undulations in the local landscape as the ground suddenly folds beneath forcing the road to lift you up to enjoy an even finer view of the river. The route is laid out from Corwen to avoid the necessity of 'A' road cycling out of Llangollen but if you do wish to visit Llangollen (which is highly recommended) the road is not too busy and the distance is only short.

Access Points

The starting point of this ride is from the centre of Corwen on the A5(T). There is good car parking available nearby. You could, alternatively, start from Llangollen.

The Route

1. From the centre of Corwen on the A5(T) head north along the minor road signed to Swimming Pool past the playground and sports field and then crossing the River Dee.

2. At the T-junction opposite the swimming pool and squash courts, turn right to follow the Dee valley along the B5437, signed to Carrog.

3. Pass through the village of Carrog.

4. At the end of the village, keep to the left of the river along the narrow lane. **Note:** The whole route is along the northern bank of the Dee so do not cross the river, keep it on your right-hand side.

5. The road follows the river to the edge of Llangollen. Continue until you arrive at a T-junction of the A542, resisting all offers of right or left departures.

6. At the T-junction, turn right to visit Llangollen or turn around to return to Corwen if you want to avoid the A542 road.

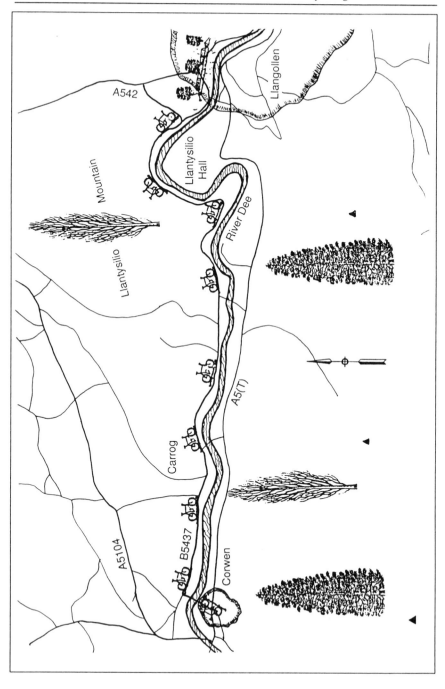

Nearby

The high ground to the north of the River Dee is the Llantysilio Mountain and the high ground to the south is the wild Berwyn Range which boasts a diverse variety of wildlife.

The bridge over The River Dee in Llangollen is one of the seven wonders of Wales. These are:

"Pistyll Rhaiadr and Wrexham Steeple
Snowdon's Mountain without its people
Overton Yew Trees, St Winefride's Wells
Llangollen Bridge and Gresford Bells."

The great old bridge is made up of four arches, each of a different size due to the construction techniques which were used at the time of building. The formers were made up from whole trees and the size of the exact arch was dependent on the size and characteristics of the particular tree. The bridge was built in the reign of Henry I (1100–1135). Builders carrying out a widening scheme in 1873 found a stone in one of the arches inscribed with the figures 1131.

Ride 18

A Circuit of Llyn Tegid (Lake Bala)

A splendid ride along the little-visited lanes north-west of the beautiful Lake Bala (Llyn Tegid).

Maps: Landranger 1:50,000 series. Sheet number 125

Distance: 13½ miles (21.5 km)

Waymarked: No

Gradients: A few climbs but nothing too drastic

Surface: Tarmac

Future Proposals: N/A

Other Cycle Routes Linking: N/A

Bicycle Hire: Bala

Shops and Refreshments: Bala

Special Comments: N/A

Special Warnings: N/A

Permits: N/A

Lake Bala (Llyn Tegid) is one of the most impressively beautiful of the North Wales natural lakes and one of the most frequently visited. It is over 4½ miles in length and nearly a mile wide. A railway runs along its southern shore and the busy village of Bala is a hive of activity all year round. There is a thriving sailing and fishing centre on the lake and it is one of the very few places where one can catch the 'Gwyniad', a white scaled salmon whose natural habitat is at a depth of eighty feet or more.

Some years ago, the ride around the lake was a favourite cycling route and indeed it is still popular with traffic-hardened touring cyclists. It is not, however, any longer a safe family route which is not all bad news, because this ride around the very quiet lanes to the north-west of Bala offers a combination of a lake-side visit, excellent panoramic vistas and fairly easy and relatively safe family cycling conditions.

Bala is considered to be the gateway to some of the finest hill walking in North Wales. The magnificent twin peaks north-west of the town are Arenig Fawr (2800 feet) and Arenig Fach (2260 feet). Between them run the sparkling waters of the River Tryweryn which meets the River Dee just east of the village.

A quiet corner on the Bala ride

Access Points

There are three main car parks in Bala, two of them at the north-eastern end of the lake. These directions assume you are leaving from the centre of Bala village on the A494(T). There are two very short stretches of 'A' road but the conditions are good and there are no blind corners. Most of the route follows quieter minor and 'B' roads.

The Route

1. Leave Bala on the A494(T) in a south-westerly direction (with the lake on your left).

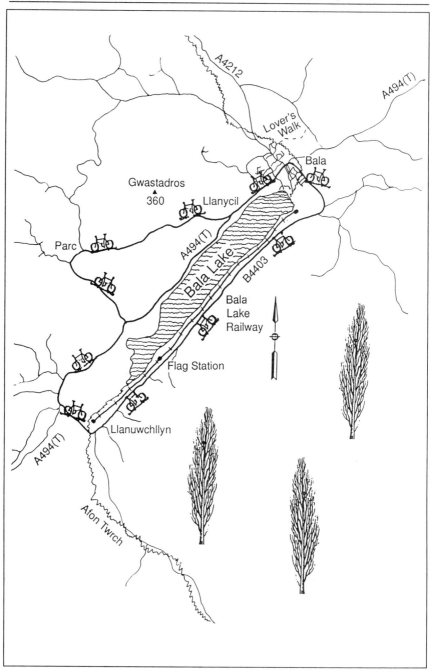

2. After a short distance, turn right onto the minor road signed to Parc.

3. Follow this road to the the village of Parc and go left at the T-junction.

4. Follow this road to the first junction with the A494(T) and turn right.

5. After some distance you will reach the village of Llanuwchllyn, turn left along the B4403 signed to Llangower.

6. Follow this through the village, over the stone bridge and keep left around the lake signed to Bala.

7. After passing through the village of Llangower, turn left at the T-junction with the B439 to return to Bala.

Nearby

The Rheilffordd Llyn Tegid (Bala Lake) Narrow Gauge Railway runs from Pandy, south-west of the lake to Bala Station at the north-eastern tip of the lake. Originally an abandoned standard-gauge route, it was resurrected in 1972 as a narrow-gauge tourist route running a mixture of diesel and steam locos. The scenic $4\frac{1}{2}$ mile run takes about twenty-five minutes each way and is a splendid way to waste away a wet afternoon.

The waters of the River Tryweryn were used to great success in 1981 as the venue for the Canoe World Slalom and Wild Water Racing Championships. The national white water centre is based in Bala. Other activities around Bala include wind surfing, sailing, pony trekking, and, each November, the Llyn Tegid Cycling Road Race.

Ride 19

Bala and Llyn Celyn

A superb circular tour around the quiet backwaters of Llyn Celyn and the little lanes north of Bala.

Maps: Landranger 1:50,000 series. Sheet number 125

Distance: 19 miles (30.5 km)

Waymarked: No

Gradients: The general trend is downwards to Bala and up again to return to Llyn Celyn. There are no heartbreaking climbs, most of the way the gradient is very gradual

Surface: Tarmac minor road

Future Proposals: N/A

Other Cycle Routes Linking: Ride 18 (Llyn Tegid)

Bicycle Hire: Bala

Shops and Refreshments: Bala

Special Comments: N/A

Special Warnings: N/A

Permits: N/A

This superb ride follows around the surprisingly gentle slopes of the quiet lanes north of Bala and around the peaceful waters of Llyn Celyn Reservoir. Situated in the shelter of the great peaks of Arennig Fawr (2800 feet) and Arennig Fach (2260 feet), the lovely waters of Llyn Celyn are retained by a sweeping dam at its eastern end. The ride traces around the reservoir and descends into Bala before returning to the lakes car park via the valley of the Afon Tryweryn.

This ride falls within the boundary of the Snowdonia National Park and takes you a grand variety of scenery, ranging from unfenced moorland road to lush mossy wooded valleys with rocky tributaries. There is always a good chance to see a range of wildlife in this sort of mixed rural environment and if you have time to linger, there are some great views.

Bala is a very pleasant touring centre and there are many interesting shops which are well worth visiting. For keen anglers, Bala offers a special treat in the form of the 'gwyniad' salmon. This white-scaled deep-water variety of salmon lives at depths of eighty feet or more and can only be caught by specialised techniques.

Access Points

There is car parking either side of the dam at Llyn Celyn and by starting the ride from here in the suggested anti-clockwise direction, you will benefit from a downhill run on the unavoidable section of 'A' road. To get to the car parks, take the A4212 out of Bala.

Early morning behind Llyn Celyn

The Route

1. From the car parks by the dam on Llyn Celyn, turn left along the A4212 heading west.

2. After following around the reservoir for five miles, you will arrive at the end of the reservoir. Turn left into the minor road signed to Arenig Llidiardau and Rhyd-uchaf.

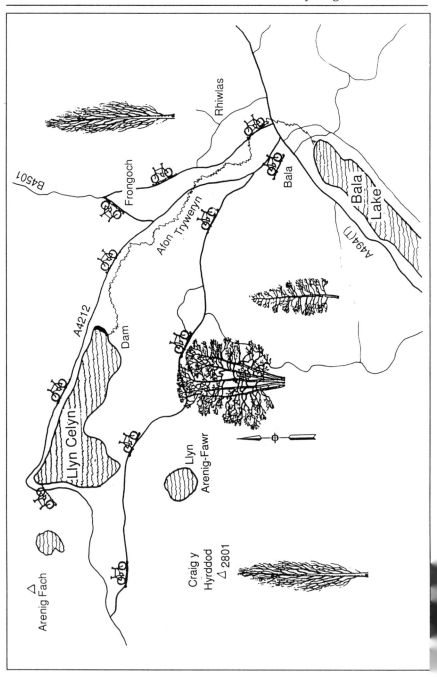

3. After about four miles, passing over some cattle grids and leaving the reservoir behind a hill, pass through the village of Llidiardau.

4. After passing through Rhyd-uchaf, he road rises for a while before leading to the junction with A4212 on the edge of Bala. Turn right and drop down into the town.

5. Turn left along the main street in Bala and follow the A494(T) to the edge of the town over the stone bridge.

6. Immediately after crossing the bridge, take the left turn just beyond the impressive arched gateway signed to Rhiwlas.

7. Follow through the attractive wooded area and you will soon have enjoy excellent views over the Afon Tryweryn valley to the left.

8. At the T-junction with the B4501, turn left.

9. At the T-junction with the A4212, turn right and follow the road through the village of Frongoch to return to the car park.

Nearby

Llyn Tegid (Bala Lake) is the largest of the natural lakes in this North Wales region. Apart from angling, the lake has become a very popular centre for other forms of water activity including canoeing and diving. More sedate activities that may be pursued in the area around the lake include painting and pottery.

In total it covers 1,084 acres and extends to over 4 miles in length. The deepest parts go down to over 150 feet in places while much of the soft shore is often quite shallow for some distance before suddenly plummeting to great depths.

Ride 20

The Afon Artro Valley: Shell Island to Llyn Cwm Bychan

A simple and tremendously enjoyable ride from the tidal causeway at Shell Island, up a pretty rocky river valley to a peaceful lake side haven.

Maps: Landranger 1:50,000 series. Sheet number 124

Distance: 17 miles (27 km)

Waymarked: No

Gradients: Easy

Surface: Tarmac minor road

Future Proposals: N/A

Other Cycle Routes Linking: N/A

Bicycle Hire: Harlech

Shops and Refreshments: Limited to Llanbedr and Shell Island

Special Comments: N/A

Special Warnings: N/A

Permits: N/A

Some of the best bicycle rides are no more than a ride up and down the road. This ride is precisely that, a delightfully easy 8½ mile stretch up the road and an even easier 8½ miles back, following the rock strewn River Artro inland from the delightful promontory known as Shell Island and culminating at the magical calm and peace of the waters at Llyn Cwm Bychan.

The route inland from Llanbedr follows an absolutely lovely mossy valley with crystal stream beds, large undisturbed boulders and slabs of clean rock scattered over the surrounding landscape. The route seaward from Llanbedr follows a short but fascinating road past a military air station and onto a causeway to Shell Island and its clean sandy beach.

This is an ideal ride for a sunny day when the good availability of shade and the constant presence of cool inviting water will counteract the effects of a hot sun.

Access Points

From the A496 in Llanbedr, follow the sign towards the airfield and Mochras. Cross the level crossing by Llanbedr station and continue as far as possible, subject to tidal considerations. If the tide is out, the causeway can be crossed safely but if the tide is in (or coming in) beware; you, or your car, may become marooned. Tide tables are usually available at local shops.

Time and tide . . .

The Route

1. Cross the causeway from Shell Island towards Llanbedr, passing the airfield on your right. Note the 'Beware of low flying aircraft' signs.

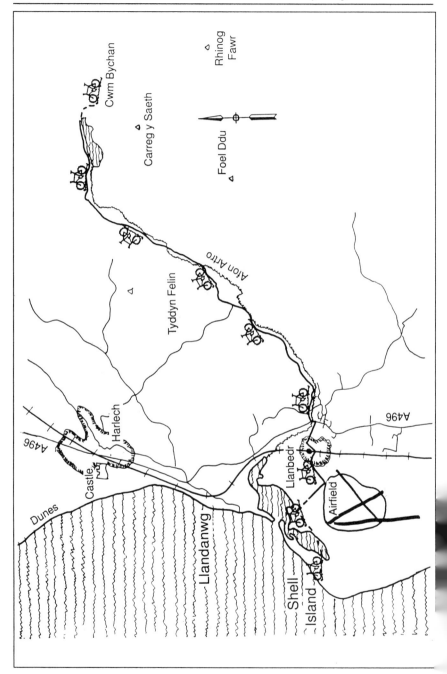

2. After crossing the level crossing into Llanbedr, turn left at the T-junction and cross the old stone bridge.
3. Turn immediately right signed to Cwm Bycha'.
4. Continue along this road until you arrive at Llyn Cwm Bychan.
5. Turn around and retrace your route to Shell Island

Nearby

Shell Island, or to give it its proper name, Mochras, is a delightful promontory of mainland coast which becomes isolated from Llanbedr and the local road system at high tide when the causeway is covered. There is a clean sandy beach which, apart from being great for bathing and sun seeking purposes, offers an enormous variety of shells, especially after stormy weather conditions. If you find yourself cut off on the island by the tide, make the most of your time there by collecting as many different shell species as you can before the tide turns to allow you back to full civilisation. In all over eighty different types have been found.

Ride 21

Llanfachreth and Coed-y-Brenin Forest

A ride around the lovely lanes of the Coed-y-Brenin forest, based on the delightful unspoilt village of Llanfachreth.

Maps: Landranger 1:50,000 series. Sheet number 124

Distance: 8 miles (13 km)

Waymarked: No

Gradients: A climb back into Llanfachreth but the rest of the route is either downhill or fairly even.

Surface: Tarmac and well-drained solid forestry track

Future Proposals: N/A

Other Cycle Routes Linking: Ride 22 (A short rural circular from Llanfachreth)

Bicycle Hire: Dolgellau

Shops and Refreshments: Llanfachreth

Special Comments: N/A

Special Warnings: N/A

Permits: N/A

Llanfachreth is a beautifully unspoilt village in the high ground north of Dolgellau. This ride centres on the village and visits a glorious part of the Coed-y-Brenin forest via the Precipice Walk. The Precipice Walk is the description given to a high ridge two miles north of Dolgellau from where there are magnificent views across the Cambrian Mountains, including the peaks of Aran and the rocky face of Cader Idris which rises to nearly 3000 feet above the sea.

This ride visits a very picturesque part of the forest and combines the minor road system with a lovely short cut along a forestry road, to return along the other side of a woody valley. There is a short sharp climb to return to Llanfachreth but apart from that there is no major difficulty. The forestry section of the ride passes through mossy valleys amid a profusion of colour, water and fantastic woodland scenery.

Coed-y-Brenin
Forest

A470(T)

Llanfachreth

Arboretum

Enjoy the thrill of the views from the Precipice Walk. In certain places, those not happy with heights would be well advised, "Don't look down!" There are plenty of interesting spinneys and old stream bridges. At the end of the route it's worth a little extra effort to climb the last half mile or so into Llanfachreth.

Llanfachreth

Access Points

The directions are given from the centre of Llanfachreth and as there is good car parking in the village. A very good alternative to the Llanfachreth starting point would be the National Trust car park at the beginning of the precipice walk. From there go left and follow the route directions given.

The Route

1. From the centre of Llanfachreth by the road fork by the war memorial, head down hill signed to Dolgellau and Llwybr Cynwch (Precipice Walk).

2. Turn right by the NT car park signed to Hermon and Llwybr Cynwch.

3. After descending into the beautiful wooded valley by the waterfall, carry straight on at the crossroads signed to Abergeirw.

4. After following along the valley's edge for a while turn left at the T-junction by the phone box.

5. After a short distance, turn left along a forestry track.

6. When you reach the tarmac road again, keep left.

7. Go left at the T-junction and follow the sign to the forest garden.

8. Go straight on at the crossroads up the single track road for the climb back up to Llanfachreth

Nearby

Cader Idris (2927 feet) is a magnificent mountain, and although not the highest in the area (Aran Fawddwy is 2970 feet), it has an imposing presence that has earned it a special place in the hearts of mountain lovers. According to local myth one of three things may happen if decide to sleep the night on Cader Idris. You will wake up either blind, mad or as a poet.

Llyn Cau, a lake at the base of Cader Idris, also has its fair share of myth which includes the story that it is bottomless and is home to a monster worthy of residence in Loch Ness.

Ride 22

Llanfachreth

An easy short rural circular ride from the unspoilt village of Llanfachreth.

Maps: Landranger 1:50,000 series. Sheet number 124
Distance: 6 miles (9.5 km)
Waymarked: No
Gradients: Easy
Surface: Tarmac country lanes
Future Proposals: N/A
Other Cycle Routes Linking: Ride 21 (From Llanfachreth into the woods)
Bicycle Hire: Dolgellau
Shops and Refreshments: Llanfachreth
Special Comments: An easy ride, suitable for supervised small children
Special Warnings: N/A
Permits: N/A

This is an easy and very pleasant rural circular ride based on the beautiful unspoilt village of Llanfachreth. There are great views, both long distance and local and the gentle farmland combines with old broadleaf woodland features to provide a most fascinating and relaxing outing. This is an ideal family ride.

This very easy ride enjoys solid, smooth and well-drained country lanes. Although short, the route is varied and interesting in both wildlife and industrial archaeological senses. Here are the complete ingredients for pleasurable virtually traffic-free cycling, all set in the magnificence of some of the most beautiful river valleys and estuaries of this scenic North Wales area.

For fitness purposes, this route offers enough gradient to be suitable for personal training by riding against your own time targets. To make the best out of time training, set yourself an easy benchmark time by riding the route once at a normal, fairly leisurely pace. Try to improve your time by a small margin on each subsequent run. Do not make the mistake of setting out at a blistering pace and subsequently attempting to better your lap. This will do little for long-term fitness and muscular strain can put your short term fitness in jeopardy.

Access Points

The directions are given from the centre of Llanfachreth and as there is good car parking in the village. Although this is a short ride, it could be combined with Ride 21 for a longer trip.

Near Llanfachreth

The Route

1. From the war memorial cross in Llanfachreth, follow the sign to Rhydymain, leaving the church on the left.

2. Follow this road out of the village and after about ½ a mile, turn

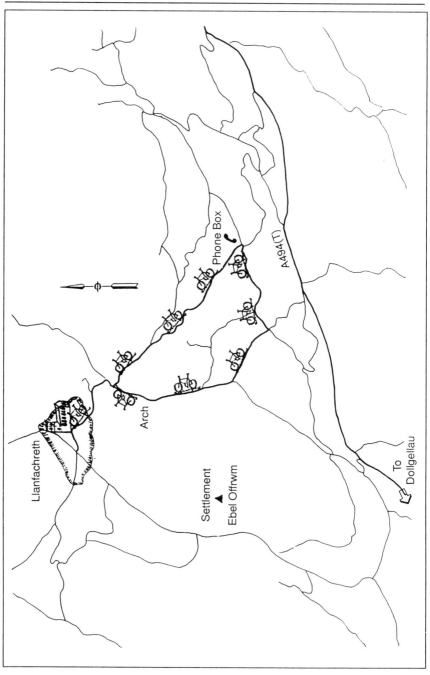

right down the narrow lane which leads under an unusual stone archway.

3. After passing under the arch, keep right at the first Y-junction.
4. Go left at the second Y-junction signed to Bont Newydd.
5. Turn left at the first unsignposted road junction.
6. Keep right at the first junction and at the crossroads by the phone box, turn left.
7. Follow this road back to the cross in Llanfachreth.

Nearby

The lovely town of Dolgellau lies in the Mawddach valley. Most of the older buildings are constructed in the very dark local slate which, although a fine and very hard wearing building material, can look a little gloomy on a dark and drizzly day. This darkness of mood is certainly not reflected in the friendly and welcoming attitude of the local people.

Ride 23

The Morfa Mawddach Rail Path

*Morfa Mawddach Station to Dolgellau via Penmaenpool. A superb,
uncomplicated ride along a level, well-surfaced recreational
railway path running along the banks of the Afon Mawddach and
the Afon Wnion.*

Maps: Landranger 1:50,000 map series. Sheet numbers 124 Outdoor leisure
1:25,000 map series. Sheet number 23

Distance: 16 miles (25.5 km)

Waymarked: Yes. The route is self explanatory

Gradients: None worth mentioning. The little trains managed it OK

Surface: Consolidated crushed stone on a firm well-drained sub-structure

Future Proposals: Constant maintenance by the controlling authority

Other Cycle Routes Linking: None directly, but plenty nearby

Bicycle Hire: Dolgellau

Shops and Refreshments: Dolgellau

Special Comments: N/A

Special Warnings: N/A

Permits: N/A

The Morfa Mawddach (Mawddach Marsh) Recreational Railway
Path runs from Morfa Mawddach Station, overlooking the sandy
delta of The Afon Mawddach, to the outskirts of Dolgellau. The
surface is ideal for cyclists, being of consolidated crushed stone over
a well-drained sub-structure.

The railway was originally built in the 1840s to carry raw materials down to the then flourishing port of Barmouth. From here,
goods were distributed to all corners of Britain and the World.

After closure, the track bed lay derelict for some time before an
initiative by local bodies recognised its potential as a recreational
linear path. With the shelter of the hills, the beauty of the estuary
and the lack of any gradients, this is a superb facility for cycling.

Access Points

Morfa Mawddach Station can be found (sign posted) by taking the minor road off the main A493 Dolgellau to Fairbourne road. There is a good car park here. The narrow gauge Fairbourne Railway crosses the estuary at this point to Barmouth. In simple terms, the estuary bridge is in two parts, one part for the rail track and the other part a promenade which can be crossed by pedestrians and cyclists upon payment of a small toll. The centre section of the bridge was designed to swing open top allow large ships to pass when Barmouth and the Mawddach estuary formed a busy port.

The wooden road bridge

The Route

There is no need for detailed directions in this case, as it is a very well-waymarked route. From the car park at Morfa Mawddach Station you will see the railway path forking away from the live narrow gauge railway to the east. Simply pedal away until you either feel like a rest or until you arrive at the far end. When you have

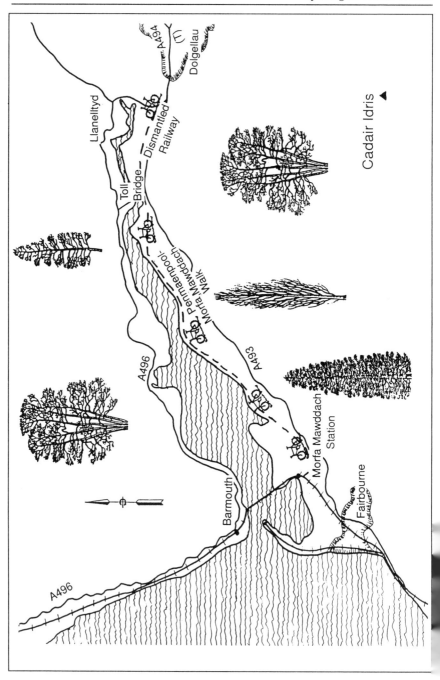

explored and seen what you want to see, retrace your tracks and return.

Nearby

Barmouth is located just over the estuary from Morfa Mawddach Station. It is a popular resort but probably more important as a touring centre for the Snowdonia National Park and all the nearby points of interest. Originally the name of Barmouth was Abermawddach (Mouth of the Mawddach River). The theory of the transition to 'Barmouth' is that 'Abermawddach' was corrupted to 'Abermo' which in turn was corrupted into a simplified 'Bermo' which became 'Anglicised' as Barmouth.

The most important historical connection of Barmouth is through Henry VII. As Henry of Richmond, he had landed in Barmouth from the continent and while planning the eventual successful overthrow of Richard III at Bosworth Field, he resided in the house known as 'Ty Gwyn yn Bermo' (The White House in Barmouth)

Fairbourne is a delightful village located on the south of the Mawddach Estuary. In recent years it has become a popular surfing centre.

Ride 24

Forest Trails in Coed-y-Brenin

An ideal family forest route plus the option of two more demanding routes through the magnificent 'Coed-y-Brenin Forest'

Maps: Landranger 1:50,000 map series. Sheet number 124. Outdoor leisure 1:25,000 map series. Sheet numbers 18 and 19

Distance: 7 miles (11 km)

Waymarked: Yellow waymarks

Gradients: There are some ups and downs but nothing too demanding or daunting

Surface: Solid well-drained consolidated forestry roads and tracks

Future Proposals: The forestry commission are committed to developing and managing the recreational facilities in the forest and have a constant programme of maintenance and improvement of the cycling facilities

Other Cycle Routes Linking: There are other waymarked routes in the forest that are more demanding than the Yellow route described here. These involve some steep climbs and difficult rocky descents that may present great difficulty and danger to the 'family' cyclist

Bicycle Hire: 'Beics Coed-y-Brenin', at the Coed-y-Brenin Visitor Centre

Shops and Refreshments: None on the route.

Special Comments: N/A

Special warning: N/A

Permits: N/A

Situated in the southern sector of the Snowdonia National Park, Coed-y-Brenin (Brenin Wood) offers some of the most glorious scenery and views in the area. Amongst the vast tracts of conifer woodland, reaching high above the deep valleys, rocky crags bulge out of the forest and in the shady protection of the valley bottoms, clear water streams over rounded boulders on its way to the sea. Coed-y-Brenin has an immense variation of growth from the more recently introduced spruce, and pine species to the old oak woodlands which trace back to ancient original natural deciduous trees that covered the area in medieval times.

Coed-y-Brenin, 'The Forest of The King' was renamed in 1935 to celebrate the Jubilee of King George V. It was previously known as Vaughan Forest after the original land owner. The timber production is in excess of 25,000 tons per annum, on an increasing rotation. The tallest trees in the forest are the douglas firs that were planted in 1942 and are reaching heights of over 100 feet before felling.

Wildlife in the forest includes a protected herd of over 40 deer which have settled in the forest after escaping from the nearby Nannau Estate in 1962–3. There are numerous squirrels, both red and grey and bird watchers should look out for buzzards, ravens and woodpeckers.

Access Points

The car park of the Coed-y-Brenin visitor centre, off the A470 (T), north of Dolgellau

The Route

Find the Coed-y-Brenin visitor centre by taking the A470 (T) north from Dolgellau. Follow the **yellow waymarks** from the visitor centre and turn right at the T-junction a few metres from the car park. This will take you in an anti-clockwise traffic-free loop on good forestry roads, keeping to the west of the A470 (T) and the boulder strewn River Mawddach and to the south of the visitor centre. (There is a short cut route which is clearly marked)

The high ground out to the west includes the Rhinog Fawr which rises to 2362 feet and, further to the south, the Rhinog Fach which tops out at 2333 feet.

Other cycle routes available from Coed-y-Brenin visitor centre, but on the far side of the main A470(T) are Sports Routes (blue waymarks) and Expert Routes (red waymarks). For 'Sports' read 'plenty of gradients, energetic' and for 'Expert' read 'rough, steep, slippery and unsuitable for normal family groups'. Maps are available from the visitor centre.

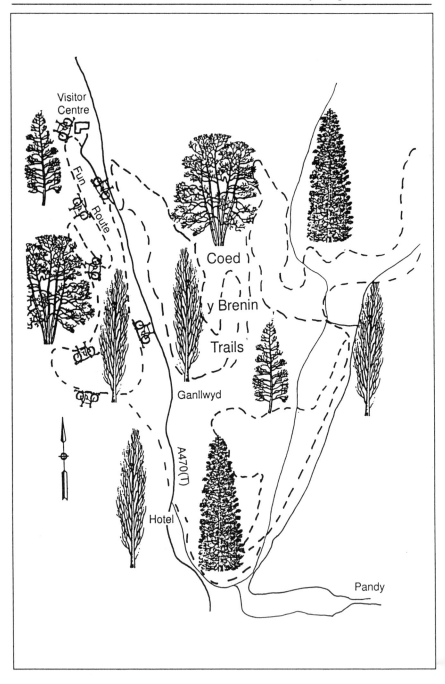

Nearby

Dolgellau is a busy compact commercial centre set at the head of the pretty Mawddach Estuary. It is a popular tourist centre and the starting point for some well known and well-established walks, notably the Precipice Walk, which circles a high ridge two miles north of the town and the short but very rewarding Torrent Walk which follows the course of River Clywedog, to the east of the town.

The Coed-y-Brenin visitor centre offers a mine of information about the forest, particularly in respect of wildlife, landscape and local events. There are toilet facilities at the visitor centre and a good car park.

Ride 25

Tywyn to Tal-y-Llyn (Llyn Mwyngil)

A ride inland from the coastal resort of Tywyn and a delightful circuit of the peaceful waters of Tal-y-Llyn Lake (Llyn Mwyngil).

Maps: Landranger 1:50,000 series. Sheet numbers 135 and 124

Distance: i. Total return ride – 30 miles (48 km)
ii. Inland from Tywyn to Abergynolwyn and the Slate Museum – 12 miles (19 km)
iii. A circular ride around Tal-y-Llyn Lake (Llyn Mwyngil) – 3 miles (5 km)

Waymarked: No

Gradients: Easy

Surface: Tarmac country lane and some 'B' road

Future Proposals: N/A

Other Cycle Routes Linking: N/A

Bicycle Hire: Tywyn

Shops and Refreshments: Tywyn plus the villages en route and Tal-y-Llyn

Special Comments: If you wish to avoid the 'B' road section, this could be treated as two separate rides i.e.: Inland from Tywyn to Abergynolwyn and the Slate Museum or as a circular ride around Tal y Llyn Lake (Llyn Mwyngil).

Special Warnings: 'B' road warning

Permits: N/A

There are two choices of road inland from Tywyn to Abergynolwyn and the Slate Museum. The 'B' road route up the Afon Fathew valley can be very busy with traffic in the summer season and although cycling is not especially unsafe, it is not pleasant. The 'back road' route up the parallel Afon Dysynni Valley, described in these directions, is the complete opposite, perfect for cycling and far more picturesque than the 'B' road alternative.

The very pleasant circular route of Tal-y-Llyn Lake (Llyn Mwyngil) is an effortless ride in the most peaceful and picturesque surroundings. The lake is popular with fly fishermen and boats are available for hire at the west end of the water. The 'B' road link between these two idyllic stretches of cycling is unfortunately and unavoidably by way of the B4405 but the inconvenience of a bit of traffic riding is well worth the trouble.

Tywyn is a delightful seaside town which is set in the delta plain of the two rivers, Afon Dysynni and Afon Fathew. The town is surrounded by mountains on three sides and with the sea to the east, there are some magnificent vistas, particularly the lights and shadows of a full sunset.

Access Points

The starting point of the ride as described here is from Tywyn. Another good starting point would be the village of Bryncrug a couple of miles to the east of Tywyn and at the beginning of the minor road section. The Slate Museum at Abergynolwyn is another possible starting point. If you wish to treat the circular ride around Tal-y-Llyn Lake as a separate ride, the best starting point is by the Pen-y-Bont Hotel at the western end of the water. Circle the lake in an anti-clockwise direction so that the water is always closest to you (as you ride on the left-hand side of the road).

Tal-y-Llyn

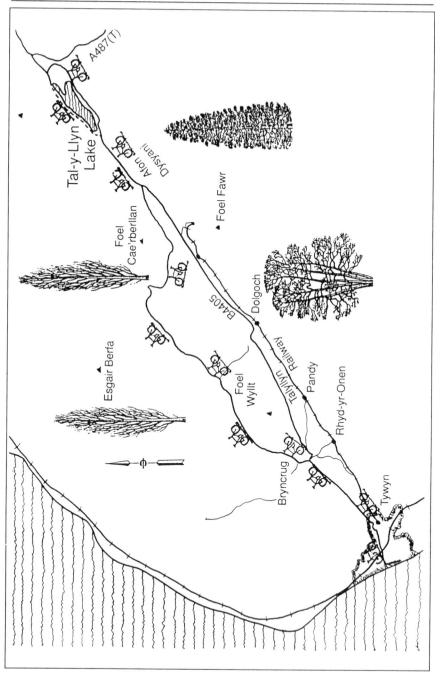

The Route

1. From the seafront in Tywyn, with your back to the sea, turn left and follow along the sea front to the new houses of the Plas Edwards development. Turn right inland here and follow the road under the railway bridge and through the town and past the shops.

2. You will leave town on the A493. Continue to the village of Bryncrug. Ignore the first right turn along the B4405 and take the second right turn just beyond the stone bridge and immediately left signed to Craig-y-Deryn .

3. Follow the road out the village signed to Abergynolwyn.

4. At the Y-junction after about two miles, keep left.

5. At the T-junction keep right (straight ahead) signed to Abergynolwyn.

6. At the staggered crossroads, with the no through way ahead, go right signed to Abergynolwyn.

7. At the junction just above the village of Abergynolwyn, go left into the narrow lane which will then proceed parallel and above the valley floor on your right.

8. At the junction with the B4405 turn left.

9. Turn left off the B4405 by the Pen y Bont Hotel.

10. Follow alongside the lake through four gates.

11. Continue through a ford before arriving at a fifth gate. Turn right here along the B4405 top return to the Pen-y-Bont Hotel along the other shore of the lake.

12. Retrace your route back to Tywyn. (It is possible to return to Tywyn along the B4405, but it is not recommended for leisure cycling. It is far better to use the minor roads from both safety and scenic points of view).

Nearby

The Talyllyn Railway runs from Tywyn, where it has its own narrow gauge railway museum, to Nant Gwernol, a total run of $7\frac{1}{4}$ miles. It was the first narrow gauge railway in Britain to be saved by a preservation society and their foresight, in 1951 while steam still ruled the rail network, was most commendable. Of the five steam locomotives, two are amazingly from the original rolling stock of 1866, the year the line first opened for business. The gauge of the track is a tiny 2 ft 3 ins (0.69 metres).

Ride 26

Corris and the Dyfi forest

*A Tarmac Forest Trail in Dyfi Fforest (Dovey Forest), and a return
ride along easy country lanes.*

Maps: Landranger 1:50,000 map series. Sheet number 124. Outdoor Leisure
1:25,000 map series. Sheet number 23

Distance: 23 miles (37 km)

Waymarked: 'Forest Trail'

Gradients: Yes, mainly at the start of the ride. If it gets a bit steep from time to time,
just get off and push for a while and look forward to the next descent

Surface: Tarmac road through the heart of the forest

Future Proposals: The Forestry Commission is committed to developing and
managing the recreational facilities in the forest and has a constant programme of
maintenance and improvement of the cycling facilities

Other Cycle Routes Linking: There are other routes in the forest that are more
demanding than the Forest Trail described here. These involve some steep climbs
and difficult rocky descents that may present great difficulty and danger to the 'family'
cyclist.

Bicycle Hire: 'Beics Coed y Brenin' – at the Coed-y-Brenin Visitor Centre, north of
Dolgellau. Also in Dolgellau

Shops and Refreshments: Corris and Mallwyd

Special Comments: N/A

Special Warnings: N/A

Permits: N/A

The ride from Corris follows a fine tarmac-surfaced minor road
through the magnificent Dyfi Fforest (Dovey Forest) winding, climbing and descending through the heart of some of the most lush and
unspoilt coniferous forest in North Wales. In the valleys, bubbling
clear streams splash over old boulders and on the higher stretches
the steep valley sides plummet down into a thick bowl of wilderness
teeming with undisturbed wild life. Points of interest along the way

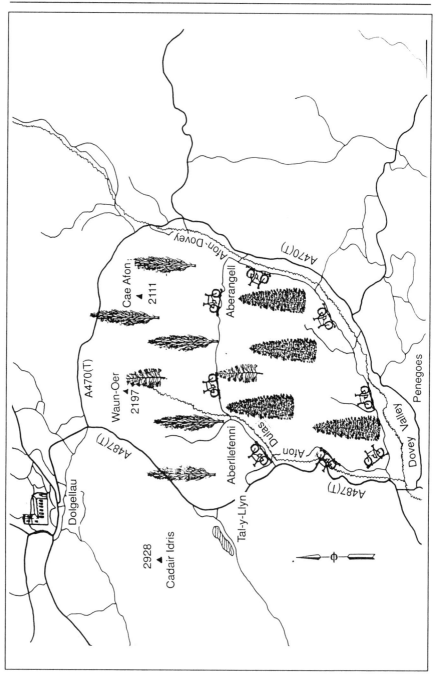

include the pretty hamlets of Garneddwen, Aberllefenni and Aberangell.

Dyfy Fforest sits high and to the north over the valley of the River Dovey. The forest has a rich mixture of conifers as well as a good spread of ancient deciduous woodland, particularly in the lower reaches of the numerous watercourse and streams. Amongst waterfalls and rocky meadows there are stunning vistas, picnic spots, alder groves and little wooden bridges that lead nowhere but the other side of the stream and past some mossy rocks.

The cycling is on good surfaces but a little effort is required here and there where the occasional steep climb is encountered. The effort is handsomely rewarded by the forest and all it has to offer. Te return rode frp, Aberangel follows very quiet riverside lanes.

Access Points

This ride passes through Dyfy Fforest and is approached from the A487(T) either via Machynlleth in the south or from Dolgellau in the north. There is car parking in the heart of the wood and in Corris.

Take the low road

The Route

1. From the A487(T) on the edge of Corris take the minor road to the east signed to Corris, Aberllefennny, Quarry, Slate Works, and Corris Railway Museum. Simply follow the road and signs through Corris and on into the forest until you arrive at Aberangell.

2. Turn right in Aberangel and follow the very quiet lane, heading south, with the river on your **left**.

3. At the junction with the B4404, go right, following the B4404 in a westerley direction

4. Shortly before the junction with the A487(T), turn right and follow the very quiet country lane to Corris, with the river on your left.

Nearby

Rheilffordd Corris (Corris Railway Museum), Corris Craft Centre and Labrinth y Brenin (King Arthur's Labyrinth) are all situated at Corris. A few miles south of Corris is the Centre for Alternative Technology where a water powered cliff railway takes you to see some clever technological solutions which use the sun, the wind and natural water as power sources.

Mallwyd is popular with writers and artists and has deep associations with George Borrow (1803–1881), who spent the larger part of his life wandering around rural Britain and later rural France, writing of his encounters and observations. One of his best known books is 'Romany Rye', a romanticised account of Gypsy life in the nineteenth century.

Ride 27

Lake Vyrnwy and Llanwddyn Village

A ride around a magnificent Lake and thoughts of buried treasures in the submerged Village of Llanwddyn.

Maps: Landranger 1:50,000 map series. Sheet number 125

Distance: 12 miles (19 km)

Waymarked: No. Follow the edge of the lake

Gradients: Not really anything worth mentioning

Surface: Tarmac

Future Proposals: N/A

Other Cycle Routes Linking: None

Bicycle Hire: None known nearby

Shops and Refreshments: In the village

Special Comments: Because you will be riding on the left-hand side of the road you will see more of the lake by circling it in an anti-clockwise direction

Special Warnings: This ride follows the public road. The traffic is usually slow moving but please take all the proper precautions for on road riding particularly with reference to the 'Be Seen' rules.

Permits: N/A

Lake Vyrnwy is the principal supply reservoir for the great metropolis of Liverpool and the original Llanwddyn Village lies some fathoms below the surface of the water. Legend states that there are buried treasures near the old Ceunant Pistyll (waterfall), which is now submerged, and that the spirits will take terrible revenge on the valley if any person tries to raise them.

The lake, as we see it today, was created by the Liverpool Corporation after an act of parliament was given royal assent in August 1880. The works commenced in 1881 and were largely complete by November 1888. The new Llanwddyn Village had been built as a part of the project and the its church was consecrated the day before the valves were closed on the run-off stream and a year later, almost to the day, the first overflows broke over the dam.

This exceptionally beautiful valley has been the backdrop for many films and forms one the Royal Society for the Protection of Birds' largest nature reserves. The surrounding hills, which are a mixture of heather and mature woodland, provide a constantly changing vista. The ride around the lake will take the average cyclist just over an hour but it well worth taking a half day over the trip and stopping regularly to take in the ever-changing surroundings.

A quiet waterside stop

Access Points

This ride is entirely on the public road. The suggested starting point is in the village of Llanwddyn where there is ample car parking. There is also an excellent visitor centre here.

The Route

Starting from the car park in the village join the lake side road. Either

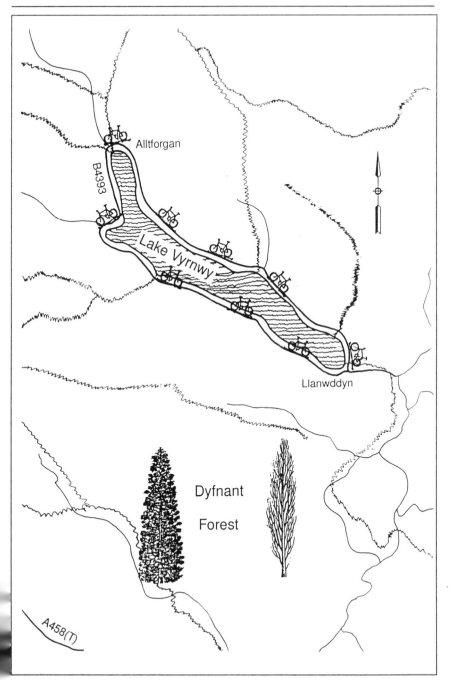

Alltforgan

B4393

Lake Vyrnwy

Llanwddyn

Dyfnant

Forest

A458(T)

direction is OK but by turning right over the dam and circling the lake in an anti-clockwise direction you will be on the lake side from your position on the left-hand side of the B4393.

Nearby

The gross capacity of the reservoir is 13,125 million gallons and daily take-off is in the region of 50 million gallons. The dam was the first large masonry dam constructed in Great Britain and led to this becoming a widely used technique throughout the world. It was also one of the earliest dams to overflow over the crest instead of utilising a bye-wash channel. The whole construction weighs over half a million tons, all built by hand. By today's standards, the building cost sounds like a bargain at only £620,000.

The 'New Village' of Llanwddyn is now over a hundred years old and has a mellowed nicely into maturity. There are good car parking facilities and refreshments available. Call in at the lake visitor centre and enjoy the impressive 'sight and sound experience' in the exhibition. There is also a mass of information about the lake and the valley here. There is boat hire and a good canoeing centre in the village.

One of the seven wonders of Wales, Pistyll Rhaiadr (Spout Waterfall) is the highest, and undoubtedly the most impressive waterfall in Wales with a fall of 240 feet. The water drops an initial 120 feet before hitting a step and emerging in a spout for a further 120 fall through an arch in the rock face. It is situated a few miles north of Lake Vyrnwy and is approached via a delightful minor mountain road, sign-posted off the B4396.

Although the lake was built by Liverpool, for Liverpool, it is now part of Severn Trent Water Authority. North-west Water, who have taken over water responsibilities for Liverpool from the old corporation, now only have the ownership of the supply route to Liverpool, starting at the Straining Tower which sits in the middle of the Severn Trent Water Authorities Lake.

Ride 28

Staylittle and Llyn Clywedog

A great circuit ride around the Hafren Forest and the massive Llyn Clywedog reservoir.

Maps: Landranger 1:50,000 series. Sheet numbers 135 and 136

Distance: 19 miles (30.5 km)

Waymarked: No

Gradients: Yes, especially around the reservoir

Surface: Tarmac, mainly minor road

Future Proposals: N/A

Other Cycle Routes Linking: No

Bicycle Hire: Llanidloes

Shops and Refreshments: Best to take some supplies with you

Special Comments: N/A

Special Warnings: N/A

Permits: N/A

The central features of this ride are the Clywedog Reservoir and its magnificent dam and the edge of Hafren Forest where the grassy sloping hillsides hide the headwaters of the River Severn. There are great panoramic views over the forested valleys and the miles of water and the ride makes the best advantage of the views. A little more effort than usual is required for some of the climbs but the subsequent descents are great fun and the photographs will impress your friends.

The ride is will take you east from Staylittle into the high country of the Plynlimon where, within sight of each other, two great rivers have their source. The River Wye and the River Severn subsequently flow off in different directions and have very little in common until they meet for the first time many miles to the south near Chepstow. Hafren is the Welsh derivative of Severn. This river, at its source, is

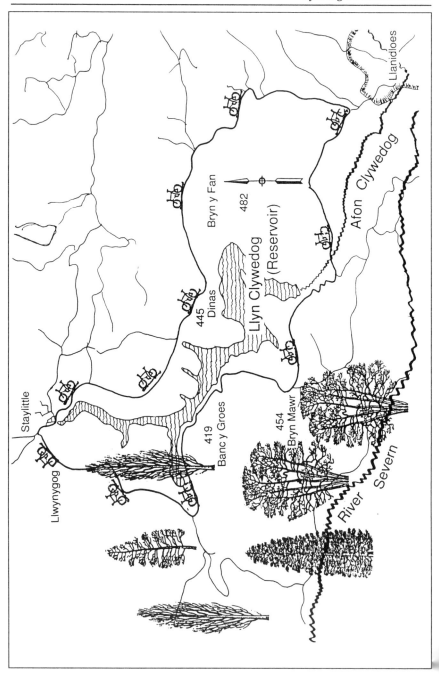

commonly referred to as the 'River Hafren', and later becomes the River Severn.

The route describes a large circuit around Llyn Clywedog, which provides water for the insatiable demand of the English midlands. The reservoir bends around the folds in the land and in all is over 6 miles in length. It is worth reserving a full day to complete this ride and it is advisable to take food with you and a camera.

Access Points

The starting point of the ride is in Staylittle village. You could also start from Llwynydog where there is also good parking. This would be a good alternative if you are planning a one way trip towards Llanidloes and prefer the idea of going mainly downhill.

The Route

1. From Staylittle, head north along the B4518 to the edge of the village and turn left signed to Llwynygog and Scenic Route.

2. Carry on straight through the village of Llwynygog.

3. Continue into the edge of the Hafren Forest.

4. Turn left signed to Clywedog Reservoir and Clywedog Dam.

5. The reservoir is a series of climbs and descents; follow the signs to the dam.

6. At the T-junction with the B4518, turn right signed to Llanidloes.

7. After about a mile, turn left at the junction signed to Fan.

8. Carry straight on through the village of Fan.

9. Turn right along the B4518 and follow this road back to Staylittle

Nearby

Llanidloes is a charming small town with an economy based on tourism and sheep. There is a lovely half-timbered market house in the central part of the town and this dates back to 1609. It is a great touring centre and a good base for the exploration of the great central reservoirs.

Above Llyn Clywedog

Llyn Clywedog is one of the most impressive of the great Welsh reservoirs and one of the most recently developed, having been completed as recently as 1967. Many local people knew the valley before it was lost forever under Llyn Clywedog and will recount stories of the area prior to the dam.

Ride 29

Nant-y-Moch Reservoir and Anglers' Retreat

*A truly superb ride around the the wild and wonderful
Nant-y-Moch Reservoir and a visit to the quiet seclusion of Anglers'
retreat based from Ponterwyd. Some fantastic ridge views.*

Maps: Landranger 1:50,000 series. Sheet number 135

Distance: 35 miles (56 km)

Waymarked: No

Gradients: A fair few climbs and descents but nothing too serious as long you accept that this is a full day's ride

Surface: All tarmac quiet country lanes and mountain roads

Future Proposals: N/A

Other Cycle Routes Linking: N/A

Bicycle Hire: Aberystwyth

Shops and Refreshments: Not much available en route but a very good 'half-way' stopping point at Talybont

Special Comments: N/A

Special Warnings: N/A

Permits: N/A

Nant-y-Moch Reservoir and Anglers' Retreat are two of the loveliest and most peaceful spots in this whole beautiful region. This is a ride around very quiet traditional Welsh mountain roads, away from the main coastal tourist centres. Based on Nant-y-Moch Reservoir, the route takes you in a wide circle and passes through a couple of sleepy hamlets along the way as well as taking in a return diversion leg to the idyllic Anglers' Retreat.

Nant-y-Moch reservoir is one of Wales' finest man-made lakes, set in the backdrop of the Plynlimon Range of mountains; the scenery is fantastic, do not forget your camera. The water from Nant-y-Moch helps to cope with the demands of the English Midlands and is used like a giant holding tank. By using rivers and an

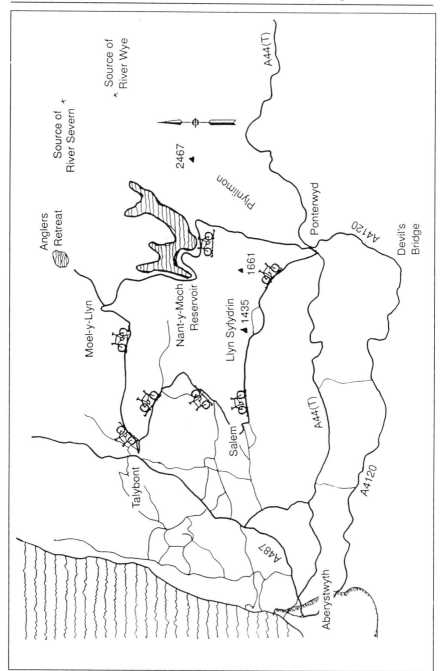

underground pipe network, water can be distributed to a range of destinations more or less by turning the correct sequence of valves. Many centres of population may draw on the water via the pipe network.

This part of Wales is well known for the tourist spots of Aberystwyth and the coastal regions but these mountain regions have just as much to offer. The A44 main road, only a few short miles to the south, carries an endless stream of traffic in and out of the this region but few people venture into the Nant-y-Moch area purely for the pleasure of a visit. Their loss is your gain, as the area provides some of the finest parts of unspoilt Wales and some great cycling.

Anglers' Retreat

Access Points

The start and finish of the ride is on the A44 at Ponterwyd. The car parking facilities near the tourist point is an ideal base point. Refreshments and light lunches are available at the Ponterwyd.

The Route

1.   At the junction of the A412 and the A44 in Ponterwyd, turn left

for twenty yards along the A44 and then right along the unsigned road by the graveyard and the school sign. At the junction shortly afterwards go straight on signed to Nant-y-Moch.

2. Continue to follow the road across the dam and around the reservoir, following the Nant-y-Moch signs.

3. After nine and a half miles, and after passing the Nant-y-Moch reservoir, on a left-hand bend is a wide unmetalled road leading away to the right. For the one way return trip to Anglers' Retreat turn right along this road and follow it for two miles to its conclusion (turn left at the T-junction of tracks). At the end of the road is a lonely little lake and not a sound.

4. Continuing along the tarmac road, after descending off the mountain section you will arrive at a T-junction. Turn right for an excursion to Talybont, Otherwise continue around to the left.

5. From here take every left turn unless it is a private drive or a no-through-route and you will return to Ponterwyd.

Nearby

Aberystwyth is considered to be the learning centre of Wales, famous for its university and colleges. One of the most famous students to attend the university was the Prince of Wales, Prince Charles. Other features of the town are the good bathing beaches, the Castle ruins and the National Library of Wales which contains 2 million printed works and 3 million Welsh historical records.

The reservoirs of Nant-y-Moch and Dinas form the largest hydro-electric scheme in the whole of England and Wales. Nant-y-Moch covers 600 acres and Dinas covers 38 acres. Both reservoirs are stocked with fish by the electricity generating company. Fishing permits can be bought at tackle shops in Borth or in Aberystwyth.

Devils Bridge is situated a few miles south of Ponterwyd and forms one of the popular tourist attractions in Wales. There are three bridges of varying antiquity built atop each other and crossing the deep and narrow gorge of the River Mynach. The oldest bridge is 12th century. Within the gorge are waterfalls, the highest of which drops a spectacular 300 feet.

Ride 30

The Elan and Claerwen Valleys

A circular return ride around the beautiful Elan and Claerwen valleys, visiting four peaceful reservoirs.

Maps: Landranger 1:50,000 series. Sheet number 147

Distance: 23 miles (37 km) or 33 miles (53km)

Waymarked: No

Gradients: Some short climbs but nothing too sustained

Surface: Tarmac.

Future Proposals: N/A

Other Cycle Routes Linking: N/A

Bicycle Hire: Llanidloes or Llandrindod Wells. Check for latest information in the tourist information office at Rhayader as there may be more local availability in the future

Shops and Refreshments: Elan village or take your own

Special Comments: N/A

Special Warnings: N/A

Permits: N/A

The well being of the Elan Valley is probably of more importance to the people of Birmingham than it is to the people of Wales although many of Birmingham's people will know little or nothing about it. The Birmingham Waterworks, which was once the pride of the Birmingham Corporation and is now managed by a dedicated water authority, is a far more beautiful thing than it appears from its dull name. The Birmingham Waterworks is in fact four large and beautiful lakes that were formed by the damming of the Elan and Claerwen valleys and are managed for the purpose of supplying Birmingham with its main water supply.

This delightful ride uses a range of easy and quiet minor roads which take you on a tour of no less than five different man-made lakes. There are few facilities along the way so a packed lunch is advisable. The views are magnificent and the purple uplands present an ever-changing carpet of natural colour as the sun alters the shadowing effects of the contours.

Hills and reservoirs are the two things that many people associate most with North Wales and what could be more hilly or have more water than this ride? Be prepared for a few climbs and enjoy the long sweeping descents and this is guaranteed to be a most satisfying ride.

Access Points

This route is described from the clock tower in the centre of Rhayader. There is good car parking available nearby. An alternative starting point would be Elan Village.

The Route

1. From the clock tower in the centre of Rhayader, head south along the B4518. Stay on this road for two miles before taking the left-hand turn towards Elan Village.

2. Keep right at the fork of roads towards Elan Village.

3. After passing through Elan Village, turn left to rejoin the B4518 towards Caban Coch Reservoir.

4. At the road junction at the head of Caban Coch Reservoir, go left for the return leg to Claerwen Reservoir.

5. Upon reaching the southern tip of Claerwen Reservoir retrace your route to the road junction. Go left at the junction alongside Garreg ddu Reservoir.

6. Just beyond the northern tip of Garreg-Ddu Reservoir the road bends left to join the southern extremity of Pen-y-garreg Reservoir. Continue following the road.

7. After leaving Pen-y-garreg Reservoir, you will soon reach the southern tip of Craig Goch Reservoir. Continue to the mountain road junction beyond the northern tip of this last large stretch water and go right to return downhill to the B4518 just west of Rhayader.

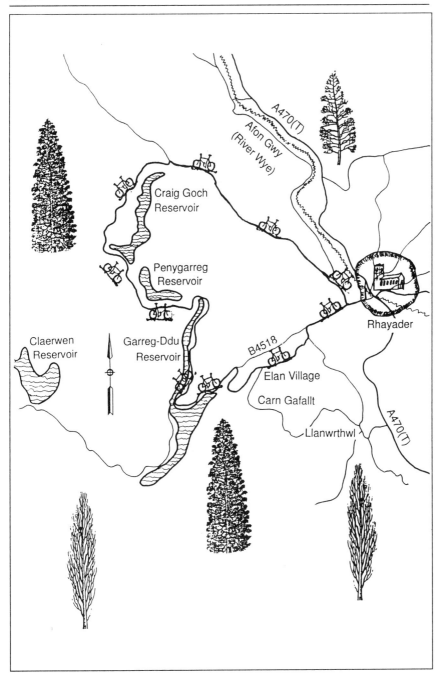

8. Go left along the B4518 for the short trip back to the centre of
    Rhayader.

Nearby

A few facts about the Birmingham Waterworks: the aqueduct system
which carries the water from these reservoirs to the city of Birmingham takes a route 73½ miles in length from the south of Rhayader
via Knighton, Ludlow, Cleobury Mortimer, Wyre Forest, Kidldermin-
ster, Stourbridge and Hagley to Frankley, where the water is stored
for distribution. Along the way the aqueduct system crosses the
River Wye, the Severn and the Stour. It also crosses numerous
streams and small tributaries.

The water travels to Birmingham at the speed of two miles an
hour, therefore taking one and a half days in transit. It passes
through a mixture of rock tunnels, steel pipe and concrete culvert
on its way and arrives at Frankley ready for purification, discoloured
from the soils along the way. The water is softer than the native
Birmingham water, a fact that was not missed by auditors who
estimated a 'soap saving' figure as a relevant effect on the local
economy when the use of this water was originally proposed.

Ride 31

A Long Tour of North Wales

The full tour, without incidental excursions onto other routes is approximately 300 miles (485 km). There are various options along the way including the possibility of exploring some or all of the other rides and on this basis, this route could form the basis of a two- or three-week tour.

Maps: Landranger 1:50,000 series. Sheet numbers. 114, 115, 116, 117, 123, 124, 125, 126, 135, 136, 137, 147, 148

Distance: 300 miles (480 km)

Waymarked: No

Gradients: Be prepared for a few serious climbs and breathtaking descents

General surface description: Suitable for any type of bicycle

Access points: This route touches on every other route in the book. Identify your chosen route by picking out the highlighted text and plan your progress from there. There are several ways to access each of the individual routes and each cyclist will have his own idea of what is best. Obvious options include transporting bicycles by car, using the various facilities on offer from the railway companies or hiring bicycles near the route.

This is designed for those who wish to explore North Wales by bicycle in one overall tour or as a cycling holiday in the area with tours between the various individual routes. To enjoy the complete tour take at least two weeks, preferably three.

The individual rides described in this book are all linked together but, because of the greater distances involved and the natural compromise of extended touring, it is not possible to avoid traffic, steep hills or uninteresting scenery to the extent of the smaller tours. Wherever possible the best route has been chosen, taking good cycling features into account, but North Wales is a hilly region.

As with every route description, an assumption has to be made that the reader is starting from a fixed point – and for this instance the fixed point has been chosen near the Welsh/English Border at Wrexham. If, however, you wish to start elsewhere, you will be able to pick up the text at any one of the 30 rides and carry on from there. I have also routed this tour to take the opportunity to visit one or two places that were not specifically explored by individual rides.

The Route

1. From the centre of Wrexham take the A525 heading west to Coedpoeth. Follow the instructions in Ride 15.
2. From the Minera Lead Mines, head south along the B5426 and turn right onto the B5605 towards Ruabon where you can join the Llangollen Canal towpath along the Ruabon Arm – Ride16.
3. Turn right at the main line junction to head west towards Llangollen – Ride 17.
4. Follow the reverse of Ride 13 to Corwen and from there take to A% heading west to the junction of the B4501.
5. Turn right along the B4501 to Clocaenog Forest – Ride 13.
6. Continue along the B4501 to Denbigh – Ride 14.
7. Leave Denbigh heading north and west along the B5382.
8. At the junction with the A544, turn right and follow the A544 for a short distance before turning left along the B5382.
9. At the junction with the A548, go straight ahead at the staggered junction to join a minor road heading west.
10. Turn right along the B5113 and follow directions to Llandudno where you can join – Ride 10.
11. From Llandudno follow the signpost to head south and make your way to Conwy – Ride 11.
12. From Conwy take the B5106 to head south to Betws-y-coed – Ride 12.
13. From Betws-y-coed, make your way north-west along the A5 via Bethesda and crossing the A55 to Bangor.
14. Cross the Menai Bridge to Angelsey and take the A5025 to Almwch. Turn left in Almwch along the B5111 to – Ride 1.
15. From Llanerchymedd near Llyn Alaw, head south along the

B5112, cross the B 5109 and continue to the junction with the main A5 Holyhead Road.

16. Cross the A5 onto the A4080 and follow this road to Newborough – Ride 2 and Ride 3.

17. Continue to follow the A4080 to return to the Menai Bridges and cross back onto the mainland.

18. Take the A487 south to Caernarfon – Ride 4 and Ride 5. .

19. After following the Lon Eifion to Bryncir, continue south along the A487 for a short distance before turning right onto the B4411. Follow this road to Criccieth.

20. Turn right in Criccieth to take the A497 to Pwllheli – Ride 6.

21. Leave Pwllheli along the A497 (the way you came). Continue through Criccieth to Porthmadog.

22. Take the A498 north-east out of Porthmadog to Beddgelert – Ride 9.

23. From Beddgelert take the 4085 heading north-west – Ride 8 and Ride 7.

24. From Beddgelert head south again on the A498 and after a short distance turn left onto the A4085, follow this road to the A487 and from there follow the signs over the causeway road to Harlech.

25. From Harlech, continue to head south along the A496 to Llanbedr from where you can join – Ride 20.

26. Continue to follow the A496 south and then east to Dolgellau. From Dolgellau look up the route instructions for these rides – Rides 21 to 24.

27. Take the A494 east out of Dolgellau to Bala – Rides 18 and 19.

28. From the village of Llanuwchllyn, at the south-west end of Lake Bala, take the minor road heading south to Lake Vyrnwy – Ride 27.

29. From Llanwddyn village take the B4393 heading south-east.

30. At the junction of the B4393 and the B4395, turn right along the B4395 and follow this road to the A458.

31. At the A458 junction continue straight ahead onto the minor road and after a short distance turn left – Ride 26 – follow this ride to Corris.

32. From Corris continue north along the A487 to access – Ride 25.

33. From Corris head south along the route of Ride 26 to Machynlleth.

34. From Machynlleth take the A487 south to Talybont – Ride 29.

35. Follow the route of Ride 29 to Ponterwyd.

36. From Ponterwyd, follow the A44 to Llangurig and the junction of the A470. Follow the A470 to Llanidloes and turn left here along the B4518 to access Ride 28.

37. Return to the Llangurig junction of the A44 and the A470. Take the A470 south to Rhayader – Ride 30.

Welsh Place Names

A great deal can be learnt about Welsh places by 'translating' the place names. Even non-Welsh speakers can deduce something from most places. For example, 'Aberystwyth' can be split into:

'Aber' – 'Where a river meets the sea or another river'

'Ystwyth' – 'Bend or twist'

So we can deduce that this place is "Where the river meets the sea on a bend or twist (in the coastline?)". Not such a bad description. Try these yourself:

Ty-Mawr; Pentre-bwlch; Pen-y-cae; Pandy; Sarn-bach; Pant-glas; Corwen; Bryn; Glan-yr-afon.

If these are too simple, try this one:

Llanfairpwllgwyngyllgogerychwyrndrobwllllantysiliogogogoch

A literal translation is: 'Church of St Mary in a hollow of white hazel, near to a rapid whirlpool and to St. Tysilio's Church, near to a red cave.'

Suddenly, non-Welsh speakers can see how beautiful some of these names are in translation. Unfortunately, not all place names can be directly translated. This is partly due to the fact that this list is purposely kept short for simplification but this is not the primary problem. The main difficulty derives from corruption of the Welsh language and the Anglicisation of a lot of the names, particularly popular tourist spots, but even in these cases, it is possible to make an intelligent guess at the meaning of the name. This list is nowhere near complete but it is enough to have a bit of fun.

Aber	Where a river meets the sea or another river
Afon	River
Allt	Cliff or steep hillside
Bach	Little
Banc	Plateau
Bechan	Smaller or less
Bedd	Grave or burial ground
Beddau	Multiple graves or burial grounds
Blaen	Extreme or furthest location. The head of a valley.
Bod	House or home
Bont	Bridge

Borth	Port or gateway
Brith	Mottled, random pattern
Bron	Slope
Bryn	Hillock
Bwlch	Pass or gap
Bychan	Small
Cae	Enclosed Field
Caer	Fortification
Canol	Centre
Carn	Promontory
Capel	Chapel
Castell	Castle
Cau	Fenced in
Cefn	Ridge
Celli	Copse or row of trees
Cil	Recess
Coch	Red
Coed	Wood
Cor	Wetland
Cors	Bog or Marsh
Craig	Crag
Crib	Summit
Crick	Mound
Croes	Cross
Crug	Mound
Cwm	Valley
Cymmer	Junction or rivers-meet
Ddu/Du	Black
Din/Dinas	Town or fortification
Dir	Topsoil
Dre/Dref	Village
Dwfr/Dwr	Water
Dy	House
Dyffryn	Valley
Eglwys	Church
Esgair	Long Ridge
Fach	Little
Faen	Stone
Faes	Field
Fan	Fenced Place
Fawr	Big, Grand
Fechan	Smaller or less
Felin	Mill
Ffordd	Route or road
Ffridd	Plantation

Ffynnon	Natural spring
Fod	House or home
Foel	Rocky or exposed hill
Font	Bridge
Forth	Port or gateway
Fwlch	Pass or gap
Fychan	Small
Fynydd	Mountain
Gae	Enclosed field
Gaer	Fortification
Ganol	Centre
Gapel	Chapel
Garn	Promontory
Garth	Hill or headland
Gau	Fenced In
Gelli/Gelly	Copse
Glan	Bank or foreshore
Glas	Blue for water or green for fields
Glyn	Glen
Goch	Red
Goed	Wood
Goitre	Home in the wood or forest
Gors	Bog or marsh
Graig	Crag
Groes	Cross
Gwaith	Work
Gwaun	Common piece of land
Gwern	Swamp
Grug	Mound
Gwyn	White
Hafod	Summer habitat, often on a hill
Hen	Old
Hendre/hendref	Winter habitat, often in a valley
Hir	Long
Isaf	Lowest point
Lan	Bank or foreshore
Las	Blue for water or green for fields
Llan	Church or holy ground
Llech	Flat layers of rock
Llwyd	Grey or old
Llwyn	Coppice
Llyn	Lake
Llys	Hall
Maen	Stone
Maes	Field

Man	Fenced place
Mawr	Big, grand
Melin	Mill
Merthyr	Martyr
Moel	Rocky or exposed hill
Mwyn	Mine
Mynach	Monk
Mynydd	Mountain
Nant	Stream
Neuadd	Grand Hall
Newydd	New
Ogof	Cave
Pandy	Woollen Mill
Pant	Valley
Pen	Top
Pistyll	Waterfall or bubbling spring
Pont	Bridge
Porth	Port or gate
Pwll	Pool
Rhaiadr	Waterfall
Rhiw	Rise or slope
Rhos	Open land
Rhudd	Red
Rhyd	Ford
Rhyg	Rye
Sarn	Causeway
Stryt	Pass
Sych	Dry
Tal	Brow or headland
Tir	Topsoil
Tre/Tref/Trev	Village
Ty	House
Tyddyn	Small farm
Uchaf	Pinnacle
Waun	Common piece of land
Wen	White
Wern	Swamp
Wyn	White
Y/Yr	The, or of the
Ym/Yn	In
Ynys	Island
Ystrad	Flood plain of river
Ystwyth	Bend or twist

Cycle Hirers in North Wales

This list is compiled from local telephone directories and may well be incomplete. For more up-to-date and complete details, contact any tourist information office. Most Forest Enterprise centres will also have information about cycle hire.

Pedalaway Cycle Hire, Trereece Barn, Llangarron, Tel: Llangarron 770357

Beics Coed-y-Brenin, Maes Gwm Centre, Ganllwyd, Tel: Ganllwyd 440296

Beics Beddgelert Bikes, Hafod, Ruffydd, Uchaf, Beddgelert, Tel: 01766 890434

Beics Betws, Tan Lan, Betws-y-Coed, Gwynedd, Tel: 01690 710766

Llan Sports, Bryn Melyn, Abbey Road, Llangollen, Tel: 01978 860605

The Bike Factory, 153/161 Boughton, Chester, Tel: 01244 317893

J.R West End Cycles, 22 Augusta Street, Llandudno, Tel: 01492 876891

J.R. West End Cycles, 121 Conway Road, Colwyn Bay

J.R. West End Cycles, 33-35 High Street, Bangor, Tel: 01248 371158

R.H. Roberts, 7 High Street, Bala, Gwynedd, Tel: 01678 520252

More Cycling Books from Sigma!

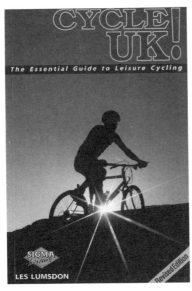